*Victory*Lap

NATHAN COX & LINDSEY COTTER

Victory Lap

WINNING THE RACE TO
AND THROUGH RETIREMENT

Published by Advantage Books, Charleston, South Carolina.
An imprint of Advantage Media.

ADVANTAGE is a registered trademark, and the Advantage colophon is a trademark of Advantage Media Group, Inc.

Printed in the United States of America.

10 9 8 7 6 5 4 3 2 1

ISBN: 978-1-64225-636-9 (Hardcover)
ISBN: 978-1-64225-635-2 (eBook)

Library of Congress Control Number: 2024900951

Cover design by David Taylor.
Layout design by Matthew Morse.

This publication is designed to provide accurate and authoritative information in regard to the subject matter covered. It is sold with the understanding that the publisher is not engaged in rendering legal, accounting, or other professional services. If legal advice or other expert assistance is required, the services of a competent professional person should be sought.

Advantage Books is an imprint of Advantage Media Group. Advantage Media helps busy entrepreneurs, CEOs, and leaders write and publish a book to grow their business and become the authority in their field. Advantage authors comprise an exclusive community of industry professionals, idea-makers, and thought leaders. For more information go to **advantagemedia.com**.

*This book is lovingly dedicated to all our valued clients,
both past and present. Your journeys, stories, and experiences
have been instrumental in shaping our approach.*

*By sharing your triumphs and challenges, you've inspired us
to think innovatively and transcend conventional industry norms.*

Contents

Acknowledgments

In our acknowledgments, we extend our heartfelt gratitude to David Scranton, whose mentorship and guidance have been pivotal to our success. We also wish to thank our friends, family, and colleagues at Advisors' Academy, Retirement Income Source franchisees, and Sound Income Group. The camaraderie and shared wisdom within this community have been invaluable in navigating the complexities faced by retirees.

Your collective contributions have not only enriched our professional lives but have also been a source of continuous learning and growth. This book is a testament to that shared journey and the lessons learned along the way.

Introduction

Are you in the Red Zone for retirement? We define this as anywhere from ten years out from your last day at work, to currently in retirement. If so, this book is for you.

The best place to begin talking about managing your money as you head toward retirement is with the basic facts of what financial planning is as you go through life, and how they change depending on where you are in that journey. Defining these basics is what this book is about. Even if you think you're somewhat clear on how retirement finances work, you are wise to read on and discover how to spot red flags, avoid pitfalls, and overcome a variety of challenges along the way. While we'll talk a little about the first stage of preparing financially for this big shift in your life in chapters one and two—the Accumulation stage, in which you acquire, save, and invest for what's ahead—most of our attention will be on the second and third stages of your financial life, Preservation and Distribution, because that's where you are or where you're soon to be.

Many people fall into the trap of thinking that if they've done a solid job in the Accumulation stage, they're home free, but that's not necessarily so. And a loss at this point is much more serious because you've got less time to make it up. Even if you think you're clear on how retirement finances work, you'd be wise to read on and discover how to spot red flags, avoid pitfalls, and overcome a variety of challenges to your nest egg as you move into retirement.

Wherever you are in your financial life, this book will help you make your retirement a Victory Lap!

CHAPTER ONE

The Life Cycles of Investing

We all recognize that our lives are made up of stages: infancy and childhood, youth, young adulthood, middle age, and old age. Not as clearly understood is that our financial lives can also be understood and managed in each of its discrete stages—what we call the Life Cycles of Investing, each requiring a different plan. People make costly mistakes in terms of their money and investments because they don't understand these cycles, they don't even know which of them they're currently in, or what investments are appropriate for each stage.

This matters because each of these stages or cycles requires a very different plan of action—and if you're not on top of it, you'll pay for it down the line. Ultimately, you want your retirement to be your Victory Lap! Let's start our exploration of the basics here.

Stage I: The Accumulation Stage

This is exactly what it sounds like: putting money away during your working years. You've got time on your side and should be using it to contribute regularly to your retirement funds.

Chances are that you're invested in the stock market, either via mutual funds or ETFs (exchange-traded funds). That's the right course at this stage of life, because should the market go down, you're far enough out from retirement that you've got time to make up for those losses. How can you maximize your efforts to save?

Get in the budgeting habit

Knowing what your costs of living are on a month-to-month basis— what you're spending on groceries, household bills, entertainment, your cars—is essential if you want to be in control of your spending, instead of the other way around. Whether you make lists on paper or use a spreadsheet, find a way that works for you so that you can see where your money's going every month. That will help you make informed decisions about spending and find places to trim the fat.

Drive down debt

Among the biggest enemies of accumulation of assets is debt. If you're in debt, and not paying it down as quickly as you can, you're risking throwing a wrench into your retirement plans. Somehow having debt has become much more acceptable to people than it was in our parents' or grandparents' generations, and people have no trouble justifying it. When we talk to clients about debt, we hear things like "everyone has a car payment" or "everyone has a mortgage," but carrying too much debt later in life is going to undermine your retirement security. A big piece of responsible budgeting for the Accumulation stage should be avoiding debt whenever possible, not taking on more than you can reliably pay off in a reasonable time and paying off what debt you have as quickly as you can.

LINDSEY

One thing I hear a lot in meeting with new clients is that they justify having a mortgage because they see their home as one of their retirement assets. That's totally wrong in some cases, because the real estate market is typically up and down, and you can't count on it being in an upswing when you're ready to cash out. If you're in the Accumulation stage, you're talking about a thirty-year time frame of looking at your piece of real estate as part of your retirement plan that you're going to sell it and utilize the profit to supplement your retirement. But an area can change a lot in thirty years, in terms of real estate value. If your home is in an area where most of the people work for a big manufacturer, that company could go out of business in thirty years, and real estate values would drop along with employment rates.

NATHAN

People will also defend carrying debt as a way in which to build their good credit. Yes, there's a value to having good credit, but as I always point out to them, if you're self-sufficient, you don't actually need good credit. Your best bet is to find a good balance between debt, debt reduction, and savings.

What's the worst kind of debt to carry? We'd say that's credit card debt because the interest rates are so punishingly high. Even when you're young and in the Accumulation stage, carrying balances on your credit cards is going to wreak havoc with your financial well-being. The costs of carrying car payments for too long mount up faster than you might think.

Maximize your match!

If your employer has a retirement plan in which they contribute matching funds for your contributions, it's foolish not to be maximizing that match, because you're leaving money on the table. At the very minimum you should be contributing at least as much as your employer will match. Say you're putting in 6 percent of your salary per year, and your employer is matching 3 percent; you're effectively getting an immediate 50 percent return on your money.

Use dollar cost averaging

If your employer offers you the opportunity to contribute to an employer-sponsored plan, use dollar cost averaging to grow your money with less risk of loss. Here's a simplified explanation of how that works.

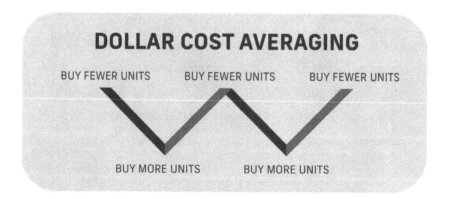

Let's say you have $100 per month going into your retirement plan. That may all be coming out of your salary, or part of it might be coming from your employer in matching funds.

Let's further say that the first month you contribute that $100, you're buying ten shares with it at $10 per share. You've purchased ten shares. The following month, another $100 goes into the account, but meanwhile, the market has gone down, and the same shares you're purchasing within that plan are now selling at $5 per share. That's a bad day on the market for your first ten shares, because they've gone down 50 percent. BUT—it's also a good day, because now your $100 monthly contribution will purchase twenty shares at $5 per share. Instead of looking at it as a bad day for the ten shares you already owned, now it's a good day, because you have a buying opportunity to purchase ten shares more. When you average it out, you now have $200 invested—but you own thirty shares. Using dollar cost averaging, that means your average share price is $6.67 per share. Remember, those shares were trading at $10 last month, and over time, they're likely to rise again to that price or potentially higher.

Dollar cost averaging lets you take the emotion out of buying shares, because it ensures you're investing in those shares regularly over time, rather than responding to every market fluctuation. And time is your friend.

Don't overcomplicate things

There's no need to overcomplicate your investment strategy during the Accumulation stage. Keep it simple, something you can dependably commit to. If you're the average investor, not a do-it-yourself day trader who wants to immerse themselves into stock market history and reports, you'll do best over time by investing in a good low-cost S&P index fund, because the S&P 500 outperforms most of the stock funds out there. Buy shares of growth-based assets; use dollar cost averaging; and maximize employer matches on your employer-based retirement fund, and you'll be making the best use of this Accumulation stage.

Stage II: The Preservation Stage (aka, the Red Zone)

This is the middle stage of your financial life: the period in which your chief aim is preserving what you've accumulated in the previous years, with an eye to retirement, which is now visible on your time horizon. You hit this stage somewhere between fifty and sixty years and continue in it until you retire.

NATHAN

I call it the Red Zone of Retirement, because in football, the Red Zone is when you've gotten to the twenty-yard line, but you've still got another twenty yards to go in order to make that touchdown. You've already done most of the work and the planning it took to get the ball this far; you've covered 80 percent of the distance. Your goal is in sight. You don't want to fumble the ball or make an error at this point and lose it. You're only five or ten years from retirement. Now it's time to transition from the Accumulation stage. That doesn't mean you abandon all the strategies that got you this far, but you need to shift your focus on keeping what you've put together.

Don't be too aggressive...

The biggest mistake people make in this stage is being too aggressive with their investments. In the Accumulation stage you can afford to take chances, because there's plenty of time on the clock and if you make a mistake, you have time to make up for your losses. But now that you're in the Preservation stage, you don't have all that time on your side, and too much risk at this point can really hurt your retirement.

...But don't play it too safe

Another big mistake is going too far in the opposite direction away from risk, putting all their accumulation in what they see as ultra-safe, risk-free accounts. Now, they're making no return on their assets. That's not good either.

Know when it's time to change your strategies

The third error people make is not realizing that they've actually hit the Preservation stage. They stay in the Accumulation stage mindset, taking unnecessary risks to accumulate more. They don't think they have enough. Some folks have lost money or failed to save enough, and they're having to play catch-up.

LINDSEY

This is something we discussed on our Retirement Income Source radio show recently: how some people stay in the Accumulation stage too long because they don't think they have enough—but what exactly is enough? We find that a lot of people aren't clear on what "enough" is. The fact is, some of them have already won the game, and just don't know it.

> **NATHAN**
>
> I saw this with a good friend of mine. He'd worked for the family business for thirty years; he'd accumulated half a million dollars in assets and in his 401(k), and between his income and what he'd saved, he could have retired comfortably with no change in his lifestyle. But he was working with an advisor who pushed him to stay in growth-focused investments, and in the Accumulation stage. In 2008 the market had a huge correction. He was pulling money out of his funds; the market recovered, but he never did.

What's the last reason people stay in the market too long? Is it greed, or just habit? For some folks, enough is never enough. That's a piece of who they are, and there's no way to convince them to change. Others enjoy an element of risk for its own sake. Either way, it's an emotional relationship with money, rather than a rational, realistic one.

Have a realistic relationship with your money

One of the things that complicates planning for retirement is not understanding what your expenses will be. Many people make the error of assuming that their expenses will go down, but in reality that's often not the case. Many also assume that if their spouse passes, they will only need half as much money as they did as a couple, but that isn't the case. Sometimes pensions don't come with survivor benefits; in other cases, people may not have elected survivor benefits in their pension plans. It also depends on Social Security and choosing the best time to claim that.

One of the main components is ensuring that your assets are allocated properly, in such a way that will allow you, during this particularly critical life stage, to keep your principal intact as you then move into the Distribution stage. Recognizing this relationship with your savings and developing the proper strategy will also allow you to build up the amount of income this money will generate for you.

Stage III: The Distribution Stage

Congratulations! You've made it to the finish line of your working life—retirement—and are ready to enjoy the fruits of your labors. That said, you still need to understand the stage you're in, and take appropriate steps to guard and invest in your nest egg.

Know where your money is, and what it's doing for you

As in all things financial, knowledge is power. We recently did a retirement workshop for a large group. Two ladies stayed behind after the rest of the people had left. One of us went to them to ask what they needed, and one of the ladies said, "I really feel like I need to schedule a consultation with you to talk about my money, because I'm going to be retiring in a couple of months—but I don't know what I have, and I don't know what questions to ask."

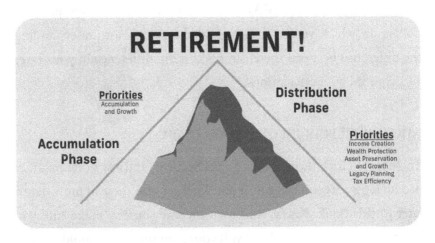

So many people we meet who are entering the Distribution stage are in that boat; they're not clear about what they have, they don't know how it's invested, and they're understandably worried about whether they will have enough to meet their needs in retirement. Don't be one of them! Situations like this are why we've created our education-based business structure: so that people are aware and prepared. Knowing what you have, and what you need to maintain your lifestyle going forward, is critical. Gather your statements together and start listing out your assets. Know what you've got, where it is, and how it's invested. And finally, don't wait until you're in your sixties or seventies! If you've got an advisor, it's time to have a sit-down with them. Ask questions, take notes, and insist they use language you can understand.

Know the difference between qualified versus non-qualified money

People can get into trouble in assessing their assets and their retirement income if they don't understand the difference between qualified money—pre-tax dollars (usually coming from an employer-sponsored retirement account or IRA)—and non-qualified money, post-tax dollars on which you've already paid the taxes. Not understanding the difference between these can make a big difference in your taxes and your income calculations.

Know what your income sources are

These would include pensions, Social Security, and any other income-producing assets you can count on. We'll get into these in more depth later in this book. Know your own income sources; make sure you also know your spouse's. What will your combined household income be? What can each of you continue to count on in the event one of you passes?

Figure out if you'll need to take withdrawals from your retirement accounts

This goes back to knowing how much income you're going to need in retirement. Will you need to access the money in these accounts early on in retirement? When you turn seventy-three or seventy-five, depending on the year you were born, you will have to start taking minimum required distributions. We've seen situations in which people start taking money out of their retirement accounts when they don't really need to, because someone told them that's what they should be doing. We've also met people who don't access those accounts when they need to, when they would have been OK doing so, unnecessarily sacrificing the lifestyle they have worked for at a point in their life when they could have enjoyed it the most. If you must take the required minimum distributions from your accounts, and you don't need the money, there are several options for you to consider. For example, you can take advantage of qualified charitable distributions, or you can reinvest the tax dollars after tax to produce more income for when you may need it in the future.

Understand the investment equation: TR (total return) equals I (income) plus G (growth)

This equation can be applied to every type of investment. The (TR), total return on any investment, is equal to the (I). How much income the investment produces plus the (G), growth, capital appreciation or loss. When you are in the accumulation phase of life, you don't care where your return comes from. You just want total return. You want to see your account balance increase. But when you reach the transition phase and ultimately the distribution phase, the whole game changes. Now you realize that you can't spend growth unless you sell something. You can only spend the income the investment produces.

TR = I + G
Total Return = Income + Growth
Bottom Line = Interest/Dividends + Capital Appreciation/Loss

Take real estate: many of you reading this have purchased real estate of some kind, most often a home. You looked at a number of properties and chose the one that suited your needs, and which you believed would grow in value over time. You're not making money off of it; you're not renting it or farming on it (it's not producing any income). You're buying it and holding it. Alternatively, you might take that same money and invest it in, say, farmland, and lease it to a farmer for a regular fee. Now, that property may go up or down in value—and in the meanwhile, it's producing income. Over time, the income it produces plus whatever its increase in value equals your total return. If you then take that lease money and reinvest it, you can further increase your total return. What's the best choice? There is no single answer. It all depends on where you are in your financial life and what your needs are.

Bottom Line

Make no mistake: you are the one ultimately in charge of your financial future. But you can't control what you don't know about—so you need to understand the Life Cycle of Investing and your place in it, in order to be in control when it comes to your money. In the next chapter we'll talk about some of the most dangerous mistakes we've seen folks make in these and other areas that can wind up torpedoing retirement plans.

CHAPTER TWO

Getting Past Retirement Pitfalls

Over the years that we've been advising folks on how to optimally plan for a secure and comfortable retirement, we've met all kinds of people: people who've put a lot of thought and research into their financial planning, those who've given it some attention and done some planning, and many who have simply let it slide and hoped for the best.

But anyone, no matter how savvy they are or how good they are about adding to their nest egg regularly during their earning years, can make mistakes—and many of the seemingly small mistakes they make can have damaging repercussions for their financial health down the line. In this chapter we'll examine some of the most common pitfalls and talk about how you can make your way safely around them.

The Pitfall: Failing to Plan

Failing to plan is—well, planning to fail. If there's one time in your life you don't want to fail, it's certainly in your retirement years. Yet many people, even those who have managed to put money away in retirement accounts through their working years, wind up with less income than they need, all because the way in which they invested wasn't the optimal choice for them.

Even if you have planned and taken the best advice you could find on where to invest, you still need to revisit that plan as time passes. Things change, and your planning and investments need to change along with your needs, your marital or health status, or the many other events that can impact your needs.

We see this much too often; people have planned using outdated assumptions about their needs that no longer fit their situations, and the price for that comes due when they can least afford it—at the point they're ready to retire. Sadly this happens very often in situations when one of the partners in a marriage passes away, upending the family finances in ways that the surviving spouse didn't see coming. Most often what we see is the wife being the surviving spouse.

One lady we worked with recently found herself in this position when her husband passed unexpectedly. She had claimed her Social Security early, and the two of them had anticipated claiming his later when he'd reached his full retirement age. Unfortunately, he didn't make it. They had assumed that they'd have both of these monthly income sources coming in, and that those would be sufficient to support them in retirement. Now, with the reduced amount she was going to get, she saw that income stream cut almost in half. In addition, they had significant debt they were still paying on when her husband passed.

They thought they had a retirement plan—but they hadn't considered the ways that plan could be torpedoed by something unexpected like the husband's death, and now his widow was looking at a very bleak financial future. Ultimately, she had to go back to work as a babysitter and worked well into her seventies.

The way around

Find a good advisor early on, ideally when you're still in the Accumulation stage. Your advisor should have the heart of a teacher and a true understanding of investments at different stages of life. Listen to what they tell you. Continue always to listen and ask questions as the years go by and your goals change, because as we learned in chapter one, as you near retirement and eventually enter your Distribution stage, your investment strategy needs to change along with the stage you're in.

We understand why some folks fail to plan. Most of us lead busy lives, with different demands on our time, both personal and professional. But letting your financial future effectively take care of itself is a very bad idea. Unfortunately for this lady, because she didn't seek our help until after her husband had died, there was very little we could do for her, but we did what we could. She had to take less income from her investments than she'd wanted to, to preserve the principal, because she needed to preserve what she still had. We can't go back in time and fix what could have been. Instead, we focused on making the best of what she had to create the best retirement possible.

The Pitfall: Having a "Magic Number"

People read articles or listen to financial pundits that put forward a "magic number"—the amount you must have to be secure in retirement—and take them as gospel. This can either lull them into a false sense of security or cast them into despair since they don't see any way to hit that number. The fact is, there IS no magic number—and there are multiple ways to get where you need to be for financial security that don't rely on magic numbers.

Many people are fixated on that $1 million or $2 million mark—"If I just have a million dollars, I'll be fine"—but that number was assigned in their minds thirty years ago. What a million dollars could buy thirty years ago is much less than what it can buy now, and certainly will be worth even less over the next twenty to thirty years.

The magic number people have in their heads varies to some extent depending on what they see as their guaranteed income sources, but the generation that could usually depend on at least one lifetime pension as an income stream is shrinking. The bigger point is that there is no one number that fits all circumstances, lifestyles, or needs.

The way around

Recognize that there is no reliable "magic number" that will guarantee your financial security in retirement, and plan accordingly. OK, maybe Jeff Bezos can relax, but for the rest of us, we're better off being fully aware of what our income in retirement will look like, and how best to invest the money we've put away.

Ask yourself this question: What is the purpose of the money I have saved? Is the purpose to take a lump sum withdrawal and buy a boat or a vacation home? Is the purpose to live a very thrifty, simple lifestyle so I may leave a legacy for my family? Is the purpose of the money I have saved to provide income and financial security in retirement? If the purpose of the money you have saved is income, doesn't it make sense that the investments should match that purpose? Security in retirement isn't only or even primarily about what your portfolio value is, it's the amount of income it can generate, because ultimately that's the purpose of it.

It all comes down to knowing what you need to have the lifestyle you want. What are your individual needs and goals? Do you want to travel extensively in retirement? Do you want to leave your children or a favorite charity a sizable legacy? Depending on where and how you live, you might require $40,000 in income a year to live comfortably, where another person with different wishes may require $200,000 to meet their needs. Knowing the numbers and planning your budget to cover them will get you where you want to be.

LINDSEY

People tell me they're frugal, but when we talk about what that looks like in practice, they may enjoy expensive hobbies or getting a new car every year and they need at least $70,000 a year income above and beyond their Social Security to continue that lifestyle. Well, heck that's not frugal compared to the person that's cutting coupons, is it? Someone else's version of frugal isn't a realistic yardstick against which to measure your needs. These things are very individual.

The Pitfall: DIY Retirement Planning

Bright, capable people tend to assume that they're equally skilled in all areas of life and often opt to do their own retirement planning—sometimes with disastrous results. Why? Because it's not as simple as it looks, and the many, ever-changing variables that affect your retirement nest egg all need to be accounted for.

We recently met with a gentleman who had gone that route without any financial guidance from anyone apart from his 401(k) provider (which in our opinion doesn't really count as "guidance"). He had suffered significant losses to his nest egg during the market debacle in '08/'09, when his retirement was still many years off. He didn't want to lose any more of it, so he pulled the bulk of it out of the markets and instead chose to put it into cash or cash-like instruments, such as money market funds and CDs. Because of that choice, he'd made very little on his money, and his timidity regarding the market meant he had missed the chance to grow his portfolio into what he needed it to be. Now, this was a smart guy with a degree in finance, who'd had a career in contract bidding for a large company, working on multimillion-dollar mergers, and he was very good at his job. But all that financial acumen didn't help him when it came to his investments. He had an emotional connection to his money and let emotion drive his financial decisions. He'd been too conservative.

Being too aggressive in investing is another mistake we frequently see made by people who are going the DIY route. A lot of these investors have FOMO, "fear of missing out." They see the market gaining and invest too much into growth-focused investments. They lose sight of the purpose of the money. This can have devastating results.

The way around

Start by asking yourself this simple question: Would you do your own appendectomy? Certainly, you'd save some money, but there are times in life when having an expert working for you is the only smart choice, and retirement planning is one of them.

The thing about the rules for retirement planning is that they change, month to month, year to year, and certainly stage to stage. There are too many moving parts for non-professionals to keep up with. Tax laws change, and rules regarding retirement investments change. The market shifts, interest rates rise or fall. New investment products become available; some of them good, some of them not so good, but all marketed to dazzle an individual investor into buying them. Colleagues or friends often offer free advice—which is all too often worth exactly what you pay for it. Why put your future at risk, when an investment expert can protect you from the pitfall of unnecessary losses? Put down the scalpel; call the surgeon instead.

The Pitfall: Assuming Your Plan Means You Can "Set It and Forget It"

Even if you've had a planner in the past, and conscientiously left your investments where they were put years ago, things change. You may assume that your money is working for you and remains effective where it is, but unfortunately retirement plans aren't "set it and forget it"— they need regular reviews and possibly revisions to work their best.

NATHAN

Some years back, we had a couple come to see us, both in their late sixties. A disability had forced the wife to retire at sixty-five, but her husband was still working. She had a big cardboard file box with her that contained the statements from the brokerage account they had with a well-known firm. They had lost a lot of money, she explained, which was why her husband had had to go back to work. I went through the statements and noted that two years previously they had had enough money to produce sufficient income for them both to retire. I asked the husband what he thought had happened. He shook his head and told me they'd been with the same advisor for twenty years and didn't understand what had gone wrong.

I could see what had gone wrong, though; that advisor had been using the same investment strategy for twenty years—from when the couple had been in their forties to the present time, when they were in their sixties. There was no change in how their money had been invested. When I asked them, they admitted that they'd never taken the time to really review their portfolio, or to meet with him to discuss it. They'd talked on the phone with him every few years but that was the extent of their input because they honestly didn't want to stress out over market fluctuations. Now they'd paid for that choice with their financial security in retirement, because they were forced to take withdrawals by selling shares that eroded their principal.

We see it over and over in our work with clients who've gotten burned by keeping their assets mostly in growth-focused investments. Normally, when we're kids and touch something hot, we remember that feeling of having been burned, and don't repeat that behavior. But people who get burned by not having the appropriate investment strategy very often forget about it—only to be burned again when the next correction hits. Part of it is that they're afraid they've gotten behind in terms of their retirement savings and are in a hurry to make them up; another problem is that so many of these folks don't know about the other options out there that can bring them the money they need.

The way around

Check in with your financial advisor on a regular basis, at least once a year at a minimum. Bring your questions and concerns and listen to the answers. Any reliable professional will insist on this. We're committed to meeting with every one of our clients twice a year for portfolio reviews, because we want them to know where they stand, and to be partners in the decisions that will impact their financial future. Sometimes we hear, "Oh, I'm sure you're doing the right things—I'll just go with whatever you think is best." That's the last thing we want. Ignorance can be bliss, but not when it comes to your money. Then it's creating a false sense of security, and that's not being responsible.

The Pitfall: Stepping on Tax Mine

Recently we met with a couple who had done a phenomenal job saving for their retirement. Even though they had not made particularly large incomes in their working years, they'd been rigorous about sticking to a budget and putting money away. They didn't have a lot of debt and had consistently contributed the maximum they could to their 401(k) s. All their money was in pre-tax requirement accounts—and they'd belatedly realized that the required distributions from those accounts were a huge tax bomb. Why? Because those distributions would put them into a much higher tax bracket, paying double what they paid before; literally twice as much as when they were working, despite the fact income tax brackets as of this writing are at a forty-year low.

They and their advisors had been completely focused on the accumulation and the investment side of things. They should have been making financial moves to mitigate this onerous tax situation starting ten or fifteen years before they retired, but they didn't.

LINDSEY

A lady called into our radio program a while back to ask our advice. She had rolled over her 401(k) into an account at her bank. Instead of a rollover, her qualified account was rolled over into a non-qualified account. Suddenly she owed $30,000 in taxes on an account of about $150K. By the time she called us, it was a done deal, and there was nothing she could do to correct it, because sixty days had passed. The 401(k) company had sent the check to her, in her name, but it should have been done as a direct transfer into her new retirement account at the bank. It wasn't really the bank's fault or the fault of the 401(k) company; they'd just done what she'd told them to do. They weren't responsible for warning her about the tax consequences.

The way around

Don't make any money moves without thoroughly understanding the tax consequences before you make the changes. While we're all in favor of everyone paying their fair share, there's no reason to give the government more than you must. We'll go into this at length in a subsequent chapter—but the big takeaway here is that not understanding how retirement income is taxed (or not staying on top of changes in tax law that can blow up your retirement funds) can cost you, big time. A tax pro can help you dodge those tax bombs and keep you from giving Uncle Sam more than your fair share.

The Pitfall: Starting Too Late

This happens all too often; we get wrapped up in the demands of work and family life, and things we don't want to deal with are all too easy to put off until tomorrow. There's always time to get around to them, until there isn't. Suddenly retirement is upon us, but we don't have a plan because we never made the time to make one. Now it's time to panic.

LINDSEY

Sadly, this is a story I hear nearly every day; in fact, nearly 90 percent of the appointments I have are with people who are retiring in the next few months but have no plan. They've saved, they have resources, but they have no idea how to maximize them to achieve the kind of retirement they want. In my view, our industry is falling terribly short when it comes to 401(k) administration. Many of them try to help guide these folks with retirement calculators and scenario planners, but honestly, it's not really their forte, so they leave the investment choices up to the employee. And the employees just don't have the financial expertise to make the best choices about where best to put their retirement funds. That can undo a lot of the good they've done by saving so carefully all those years. It's like those medical tests nobody wants to take; you can skip them, but you run the risk of letting something that could have been fixed when it was a small thing turn into a very big thing that's much harder to repair. When it comes to planning, I'd say better late than never, but earlier is better still.

The way around

Start *now*. You can't start yesterday, and tomorrow will always be a day away. Research financial planners in your area and make the calls. Set up appointments to meet with them and follow through. Find someone you're comfortable with and just get started. Create a plan together and follow it. You may already have lost ground, but despair or throwing up your hands just isn't an acceptable way to handle that. This requires initiative on your part, but believe us, it's a lot easier to take the wheel now than it will be to live your life paying for the consequences of further procrastination.

The Pitfall: Assuming You'll Spend Less in Retirement Than You Currently Do

This common mistake can undermine your planning efforts. Retirement looks different for everyone, and what one person considers a comfortable lifestyle might seem needlessly extravagant to another person. But don't assume that retirement is going to cost you less than your life does now: Most people underestimate what they're going to need.

Why not? First, you've got to factor in inflation. That's a constant, and it's going to chip away at the value of your savings.

Second, what do you want to do when you're retired? Many people tell us they want to travel, either to see the world or to visit family. A lot of people like the idea of eating out more often. Maybe what you'd really like is a vacation home where you could spend part of your year. Maybe you'd like to get a boat and go fishing every day. These are the kinds of things people talk about when they share what they dream about in retirement. But reality hits when you start adding up what any or all those things or activities are going to cost. Suddenly, you're spending a lot more in retirement than you'd anticipated.

The way around

Getting clear around your budget, your fixed needs and costs, and your wish list for retirement can help you more realistically anticipate how much income you're going to need in retirement, and where that can come from. Just don't assume it's going to be less than you're spending now. because chances are that's off the mark. Sit down with your spouse if you have one and go over your fixed expenses. What bills will you reliably have to continue paying? What kinds of plans/dreams/additions to your current lifestyle do you want to make in retirement? Look at those in terms of cost, and what they'd add to your current monthly nut. How much more would you need to have in reliable income to cover those expenses?

Next, take your figures and wish list to your financial advisor and review them together. Again, the sooner you do this, the better.

The Pitfall: Staying in the Growth Market Too Long

This is a big mistake too many people make as they near retirement. Why? Because as anyone who lived through the tech bubble blowout in the early 2000s or the housing crisis in 2008 knows, what goes up must come down. The problem is the complacency that people develop when they see their nest eggs appreciating in value—a false sense of security that evaporates immediately when the market corrects itself. We saw a flash of this in 2020, in a smaller-scale correction where some people panic-sold their holdings when they dropped, and lost money. But it will happen again—and if you're nearing retirement or in retirement, you can't afford to take those kinds of losses.

One client that went through this was a brilliant guy who'd had a long career working for a major computer company. He believed in tech—it had been his meal ticket—and had faith that it would go up unchecked indefinitely, so he stayed in the market after he retired in 1998, confident that it was the smartest choice. He got absolutely hammered just a few years later and came to us to try and salvage his retirement on what he had left. He could have chosen to double down, ride out the slide, and hope he'd live long enough to see it go back up. But that's a choice you can't afford if you're depending on those stocks to finance your retirement. In this case, the market went down in '01–'02 and took until '07 to come back—then went back down in '08 and took until '13 to come back.

The way around

If you're clear about which stage of your financial life cycle you're in, this should be a no-brainer. As we've recently seen, the stock market is a rollercoaster. Do you really want to spend your retirement years clinging to the safety bar with your eyes squeezed shut? If you're committed to staying the course and keeping your nest egg in the growth markets, you have to think that decision through; can you afford to take significant losses for five or seven years while you wait out a steep market correction? Can you afford to stop taking money out of that investment until it recovers? If you can't, let common sense and the wisdom of math be your guide. Your investments need to match the purpose of the money. The investments should generate the income you need, naturally, in good times and bad.

The Pitfall: Working with the Wrong Kind of Financial Professional

All financial advisors are not alike, and surprisingly few people outside of the industry understand the differences.

A big differentiator between financial advisors is how they get paid, because that can impact the kinds of investments they recommend. That's why it's important that you know how your advisor is paid, and by whom.

NATHAN

A man called me at the office a couple of months ago. He'd watched a webinar that we had given and he had a list of questions. He told me, "Nathan, I feel like I'm in good shape. I have absolutely no market risk. And my investment has a 7 percent guaranteed interest rate."

I said, "You have it all in one investment? How much money are we talking about here?"

He said, "Well, I retired last October. My financial advisor told me to put $700,000 in an investment account and that it has a 7 percent guaranteed interest rate."

I said, "Wow, that's pretty good. I'll tell you what; I'm an independent advisor. And I sure would like to know what that investment fund is. Would you mind sending me a copy of a statement? I'd like to look over it. Who knows, it might be a great thing! But at least you'd have a different set of eyes on that, so you could feel more confident about it."

He sent me the statement and I saw that he had a variable annuity with a particular company. He wanted to come in and chat, so when he was in my office, I called that variable annuity company on the phone. I asked them some questions, and we came to find out that he was paying 3.5 percent per year in fees, that he had no guaranteed interest rate, but he had what's called an income rider benefit. That meant that he was guaranteed 7 percent on the income benefit, but only if he annuitized the account and took the money out as income over his lifetime. This all came as something of a shock to him—all he'd heard when the advisor was recommending this investment was the 7 percent interest rate he'd thought he was getting. I don't know if the advisor disclosed all of this to him—but I can tell you people too often hear what they want to hear.

Like folks used to say, if something seems too good to be true, it probably is. And while the gentleman is stuck with that annuity—and the hefty 3.5 percent fees that go with it—he's not with that advisor anymore.

Does the perfect investment exist? Imagine for a moment a perfect world, and in that perfect world you could own the perfect investment. What characteristics would that investment have? I would imagine that investment would be completely safe, have complete liquidity and a very high rate of return. Most of us know that it's not a perfect world, and the perfect investment does not exist. Investments are just a tool to complete a task or a goal, and all involve some level of compromise.

PERFECT WORLD INVESTMENT	COMPROMISES
Safe	Risk
Liquid	Time
High RR	Low RR
Tax Free	Taxable

The way around

Your investment compromise should be the best fit for you. You've got to do your due diligence when selecting the person to trust with your investments. Don't fall for a fancy website or overblown promises that seem too good to be true. There is no one right investment that fits every person's situation. You don't need to be "sold"; you need to be educated, offered options, and given solutions that fit your unique situation. Not all advisors are willing to be able to do that. While most people in the financial services industry are good people, in our experience, some are not. That said, even the best of them can make the wrong kinds of recommendations for your specific needs, particularly if they're incentivized to sell products via commissions. So, what kind of advisor is the right fit for you? We'll dig into that in-depth in the next chapter.

Bottom Line

There are plenty of opportunities to make costly mistakes as you head toward retirement—but most of them can be avoided through careful planning. Your best bet is to start that planning process as early as possible, but if you haven't thought much about it up until now, now is the time to begin. Find a good advisor, someone with whom you feel comfortable and who's willing and able to fully answer any questions. If you feel like you're being "sold," find another advisor. And make sure to include your spouse in any and all conversations and financial decisions.

CHAPTER THREE

Mistakes Clients Make When Talking to Their Advisors

When things go wrong between client and advisor, the fault can lie with either party. A mistake overall that clients make is not being completely honest with their advisors, because withholding information can cause big problems in the planning process.

Why does this matter? Think about going in to see your doctor for your annual physical. You're asked to fill out a form that asks what seems like endless questions about your health history, your family's health histories, your habits, and any issues you're currently experiencing. If you're suffering with abdominal pain, for instance, but choose not to share that information on the form, your doctor won't know to look for the cause, and might miss something dangerous to your health.

It's the same with working with a financial advisor. We ask a lot of questions, too, when we initially meet with a new client—questions about their financial health, current investments, debts, and hopes and plans for their retirement. We count on them to answer us as honestly as they can, because the success of the retirement plan we create for them hinges on that. If they omit something that we need to know, that can undermine the very thing we're trying to ensure—their security in the future. Failing to be transparent with your advisor can be detrimental to your financial health, just as failing to tell your doctor what other medications you are on can be detrimental to your physical health. It's better to help the person who's working to help you by providing them with relevant information, fully answering questions, and disclosing information they need to know.

Understand the Basics

As the person whose future comfort is predicated on how well you grow, preserve, and generate income from your retirement savings, you need to understand the simple formula that describes how that return works. TR = I + G, which stands for Total Return equals Income plus Growth. This is true no matter what stage of your financial life you're currently in.

The balance between income and growth changes, depending on where you are in your financial life. Early on, when you've got many working years ahead of you, you don't care where that total return is coming from. You're focused on the bottom line, and you want to see it going up. In the Accumulation stage you're more likely to take risks in search of growth, because even if you suffer a loss there's plenty of time to make up for it. Later in life, whether you're near retirement or already retired, that relentless pursuit of growth isn't sustainable or suitable, because you can no longer afford the risk of heavy losses. If the purpose of the investment is income, focus more on the I and less on the G.

How this balance changes (and that it shifts appropriately to reflect where you are in your financial life) is critical to your understanding of how your financial advisor works and how to understand the advice he or she is giving you.

We'll discuss this in greater depth in a subsequent chapter, but right now when meeting with your advisor, it would be a good idea to talk over how your investment and savings portfolio reflect their philosophy regarding that balance, and what level of risks you're taking. Remember, what is risky to one person may seem perfectly acceptable to another, and that's certainly true of financial advisors.

The Most Common Communication Failures We See

Bad idea: Not disclosing a serious health issue to your advisor

If you or your partner has a major health issue that will impact your needs going forward, don't neglect to let your advisor know, because as your health changes, your financial needs will change too—and they have to take that into consideration as they put your plan together.

NATHAN

We worked with a couple over a short period of time; the husband had chosen to retire somewhat abruptly, so they were playing catch-up with making a financial plan that could support that change.

The wife had taken over the financial decisions for them both; although it was clear she hadn't had much experience managing their money, she'd prepared very thoroughly for our meeting, and came in toting a three-ring binder with all of their statements and other information in it. We noticed that he progressively took less part in our conversations, as we worked to rebalance their portfolio, but we didn't think much of it at the time, as it's not unusual for one member in a couple to assume responsibility for these kinds of decisions.

It was months before they revealed he was suffering from a terminal illness for which there was no effective treatment, and which would progressively debilitate him. You'd have thought that was something they'd have wanted us to know at the start—but they didn't mention it until it became so obvious in our meetings that it was no longer possible to cover it up. Had we known about it initially, we'd have set their portfolio up differently than we did. When we finally did learn about it, we had to do some major restructuring to get them where they needed to go—but because they'd waited so long, we couldn't achieve as much as we could have if we had known earlier.

This happens far too often.

Good idea: Calling your advisor and following up with an email, describing what the health issue is, what the prognosis is, and what you think might need changing or adjustment in your portfolio

Set up a meeting so that you, your spouse or partner, and your advisor can sit down and go over what impact this has on your planning, and how best to adjust your portfolio. Now, to clean up any confusion with what health issues are important to alert your advisor to. A good overall retirement plan will include the possibilities of unknown potential future health issues. The problem that may exist is when a health issue causes an immediate and drastic change to the existing plans. An example would be an existing planned retirement date for age sixty-seven that suddenly gets changed to retiring at age sixty.

Why would someone not disclose a health issue to their advisor? We think it's often embarrassment, linked to a fear of being judged, particularly when the issues are related to deteriorating mental capacity or other mental health issues. Some people fear feeling judged—but that's not what we're here to do. We're here to help our clients prepare for the future, which is why it's important to let us know whatever it is you anticipate coming down the road.

If you're facing a life-changing health issue, the last thing you need is more anxiety. While your advisor can't help you with your medical issues, there's much comfort in knowing that, as uncertain as the future may look from where you're sitting, your financial affairs are in order and your partner will be protected no matter what happens.

Bad idea: Not disclosing major life changes to your advisor

Divorce, the sale of a home or purchase of a new one, loss of a job—all of these can mean big changes in how you live and what your income needs will be going forward. If your advisors know about what's coming, they can help you plan strategically to minimize any negative impact and create income you'll need. Without this kind of information, they can't serve you effectively when you need it most.

Good idea: Talk over the big changes you're planning in your life with your advisor, ahead of time if you can

Why? Because not doing so can cost you, especially when it comes to tax planning, and you don't want to pay more than you have to.

Selling your home is certainly a major life change and failing to let your advisor know that you've done so can cost you. A good advisor will certainly direct you to talk with a tax advisor at that point, because you could wind up paying unnecessary taxes. And some advance planning with your advisor can help mitigate that too, so if you're considering selling, it's worth a call to them to let them know and walk through the possible ramifications. Sometimes people will think about using a severance package to pay off their mortgage, and that's also something you're going to want to discuss with your planner ahead of time. Sometimes changes in your life will mean you need to take money out of your retirement accounts, and that's also something you need to disclose and discuss ahead of time.

Are you downsizing? If so, your living expenses should go down. Alternately you might be contemplating a move that will increase your living expenses. In either case, there may be tax implications, and changes in how much income your investments have to bring in to cover your costs. If you're right on the line regarding your tax bracket, a change can put you into a different bracket—and that can mean higher taxes.

Bad idea: Being untruthful with your advisor about how much money you have in the bank

If you tell your advisor you have $50K but you really have only $10K, that may throw off the whole balance of your portfolio.

Why are people so hesitant to be straightforward about their assets when they're talking with someone whom they're paying to advise them on financial planning? Often, it's embarrassment that they haven't put away as much as they feel they should have. Other times, they just don't think to include certain accounts in their overall financial disclosures to their advisors—and that can cost them money.

LINDSEY

I'm working with a couple who have Roth IRA accounts with us, and I meet with them two or three times a year to do a review. At the last meeting we're sitting there chatting about their goals and things of that nature and the wife suddenly says, "You know, we've got $540,000 in our checking account, and we just put $200,000 of it into a CD drawing 0.8 percent for a year. Maybe that wasn't the right thing to do?" We talked about that, and afterward I went back and looked at their paperwork from our initial meeting. At that point they'd disclosed they had about $50,000 in an emergency fund in the bank, but not a word about having more than half a million dollars in a checking account. Naturally, that made a difference in their financial planning! Had they told me before, I could have steered them in a better direction than a CD making low rates.

Sometimes people are hesitant to reveal their assets because they're afraid that the advisor will insist on them putting it into an investment account that they won't be able to access. Perhaps they want to make their own decisions about that particular chunk of money and are worried that their advisor will try and talk them out of it or be offended. Most often, this springs from a fundamental misunderstanding about an advisor's investment strategy; that somehow their advisor is "putting all their eggs in one basket." But if you're working with the right advisor, they're certainly not putting all of your money in the same place.

NATHAN

My great-grandmother used to say, "Don't put all your eggs in one basket—and don't put all your baskets into one cart!" That's good advice, and it certainly applies to your retirement savings. As advisors we have multiple kinds of baskets—and many different carts.

Good idea: Full disclosure to your financial advisor from the get-go about how much money you have and where it's sitting

That makes it possible for them to help you preserve that wealth. If you don't trust your advisor enough to share that information, or if you hesitate because you're afraid they'll "make" you put it somewhere you don't want it to be, there's clearly a communication problem between you and the advisor that needs to be addressed.

It's important too to tell them if you've run through your rainy-day fund, because if that rainy day arrives and you're tapped out of discretionary funds, you may need to make some adjustments in your spending or in your investments to make up for it. The sooner your advisor knows about that, the better, because more lead time for planning can mean more options for you and a better tax outcome.

Bad idea: Not telling your advisor about other investments you have

This one is sort of corollary to the previous point, in that by withholding information from your advisor, you're preventing them from doing the best job they can on your behalf.

Why would someone not tell their advisor about other investments they have? Again, it often comes down to worry that the advisor will push them to change or sell their holdings when they don't want to. Sometimes it's a bid for independence; the client just wants to have full control and say-so over that money, without anyone's oversight. Sometimes, a client has another financial advisor and they want to keep that relationship to themselves.

But honestly, if your advisor doesn't know where your money is invested, that keeps them from doing the best job possible at creating a genuinely balanced portfolio going forward.

Good idea: Full transparency with your advisor about where your money is and what investments you already hold

Knowing what and where your assets are allows your advisor to create a well-balanced retirement plan for you, one that will address your needs and wants in retirement more accurately.

NATHAN

There's nothing wrong with having multiple advisors—several of our clients do—but consider it this way. Many people have multiple doctors. That's not a problem, but it could become one if one doctor doesn't know what medications another doctor is prescribing for you, because the wrong combination medications can be toxic. The same kinds of adverse interactions can happen in the financial world. When one advisor prescribes a particular investment, they need to know what your other advisor is doing, because a conflicting investment strategy could be detrimental to your financial health.

Bad idea: Not asking questions

Not even the best retirement advisors can read minds, and as the client your responsibility is to ask for clarification about anything—any recommendation or investment—that you don't fully understand. If they explain it to you once, and you still don't understand it, ask them to explain it again! Communication, as we have said, needs to flow both ways.

Good idea: Asking questions and more questions, because the more you know, the better a partner you can be in ensuring your financial health

We work with a wide variety of clients—some who have limited knowledge and others with vast knowledge. But if financial planning isn't your area of expertise, don't be embarrassed to ask questions. You're paying a professional not only to help you plan but to explain their choices in doing so. You need to be fully on board, so don't assume that your advisor will know you don't fully understand something, if you don't say so.

Also, don't be afraid to challenge the advisor's choices on your behalf. You're not required to agree blindly to whatever they suggest. Ask why they're suggesting the investments they are choosing, and what their potential downsides might be. There should be no hesitance on the advisor's part to talk you through these points, and honestly, you need to know those answers. But you might not, if you don't ask the questions. Remember how your teachers used to say, "There's no such thing as a dumb question." That's doubly true in this kind of relationship.

Bad idea: Engaging an advisor without knowing whether they adhere to a suitability standard, or to the fiduciary standard, which sets a higher bar when it comes to adhering to the client's interests

Good idea: Working with an advisor who adheres to the fiduciary standard

LINDSEY

We adhere to the fiduciary standard as advisors. The financial services industry has two sets of standards. There is a suitability standard, which most advisors must abide by, which means that whatever they recommend must be a "suitable choice" for the client, as generally accepted in the industry. A lot of people have this idea that if the industry approves a product or investment strategy and it's available, it must be good—which is a stretch. A fiduciary standard says you must do what's in the client's best interests; if there are any conflicts of interest, those need to be fully disclosed. The investor has the information they need to make the best decision.

Bad idea: Skipping your reviews

Not all advisors require regular reviews with their clients, but it's central to how we do business. If you don't know what your advisor is doing—what adjustments are being made to your investments—you're giving up too much of your personal responsibility for your well-being. That's a bad idea. What you don't know can hurt you.

While it's good to have someone working for you whom you trust, that trust shouldn't be blindly given.

Our clients trust us—sometimes so much that they fail to keep their review schedules. We appreciate their trust, but this is not good. People's needs and situations change; income needs change, and tax laws that might benefit them (or hurt them) change too. Pre-tax reviews are the most important.

Good idea: Insisting on regular reviews of at least a minimum of twice a year

While some advisors think that one review a year is adequate, we don't agree. Things can change rapidly in your life, and in the financial world. Reviews are the time we set aside to catch up with our clients and explain what we're doing on their behalf. They can also use that time to catch us up on events in their lives that might impact their planning.

NATHAN

I've worked with new clients and asked them, "Did you conduct regular reviews with your existing financial advisor?" And I've had people tell me they haven't heard from their financial advisor for years. There is a percentage that don't conduct regular reviews, and a percentage that do, mostly once a year. But from our standpoint once a year just isn't enough because so much can happen in someone's life in a year. That's why twice a year is mandatory for us. Quarterly is fine too. It doesn't have to be a full-on review, but it's important to touch base and go over what's happened and any changes in your financial picture.

LINDSEY

Pre-tax season reviews are particularly important because most people don't want to think about taxes until about March, when they're getting their documents together to go see their tax accountant and file. But by then, you've probably passed a point at which we could have made adjustments that would benefit your tax situation, so you may wind up paying more than you needed to. Our most important meetings are those that happen in November and December, before the year ends, and we can still make adjustments that benefit the client at tax time.

Bad idea: Not letting your advisor know how you like to communicate

Whether you're most at home with a phone call, or a text, a letter, or an email—let your advisor know the best way to reach you.

Good idea: Let your advisor know the best way to reach you and keep them up to date regarding any changes

Your advisor may need to schedule a review or have an important question to ask you—but if they wind up leaving a dozen messages you don't see or respond to, they can't do their job of advising. And keep them up to date on any changes of address, phone, or email contact information you may have. It's to your advantage to keep the channels of communication open and to be clear about them with your advisor.

Bad idea: Not including your spouse or heir in your financial planning

Most often we see that there's one person in the family who takes control of financial matters and knows where everything is. That's fine, unless something happens to that person, because there's nothing worse than being the one who doesn't know what accounts exist, how the investments work, and what the ultimate purpose of the investments are. If something happens to you, your spouse or heir is likely going to be under tremendous stress. Failing to inform them of the details is just adding to their burden at what will already be a devastatingly difficult time in their lives.

Good idea: Make sure your spouse or heir knows how to access information about your finances— and don't fail to explain to them how it all works

Take the time to explain your investments to them, show them where your financial documents are and what is in them, and make sure they understand it. Talk through financial decisions with them, so that you're both informed and in agreement. Consider bringing them along to your reviews, so they really understand it. It's to everyone's benefit if everyone is on the same page. Tasking a grieving spouse or heir with getting up to date on their financial situation when they're already emotionally exhausted isn't good planning.

Bad idea: Not tying together your retirement plan, your tax strategy, and your estate planning

So, so much can go wrong if you don't have your experts—your advisor, your tax accountant, and your estate planner—in communication with each other. Tax bombs can be set off, for one thing—and you certainly don't want that.

Good idea: Make sure that your experts are looped into each other and all of them know what the master plan is—and when it changes

This is such a critical point but so often missed! In the age of email and electronically shared documents, there should be no reason to be without a centralized hub for information regarding your accounts. You may have worked with top lawyers and financial experts for many years, but if they are not in communication, you may face a sudden and major financial pitfall. For example, suppose you bought a piece of property with a business partner and agreed to split ownership and profits 50/50. However, you never updated the paperwork after your partner got married, and the property was inherited by their spouse after they passed away. Now, the spouse has legal claim to 50 percent of the property and any profits generated from it, even though they never contributed to the initial purchase or agreement.

That's an example of a seemingly simple oversight that can happen because of a breakdown in communications and can cost your family dearly. We've seen people come in with a beautifully written will or estate plan; their financial and tax plans look pretty good, too, viewed separately. But when we look at them all together, we can see places in which each of these expertly prepared plans contradict each other and create potential for big problems down the line. More often their financial plan is in direct conflict with their future tax plan. It might be in line with their current tax plan and be working wonderfully while they're still employed and making money, but when they retire, it might end up causing them to pay a lot of unnecessary taxes.

Retirement is all about income, but more importantly, the amount of income that you're able to keep.

Very often when someone updates their will or trust, they don't realize that the financial assets they have that are beneficiary-driven are outside that will or trust, because the beneficiary asset supersedes a will. The attorney that drafted the estate plan knew nothing about the specifics of the financial side—and that makes a big mess for your heirs at the worst possible time.

Bottom line? People, Talk to Your Advisors

Don't hold back. Ask them questions and keep them in the loop with changes in your life, health, employment, or needs. Make sure the right hand knows what the left hand is doing and coordinate that information between those who are concerned with the disposition of your estate and your tax situation. Don't keep your spouse in the dark on financial matters—even if they prefer it that way. Go to your reviews! All relationships, even in business, are two-way streets. Make sure you're doing your part to keep the necessary communications flowing.

CHAPTER FOUR

What Should You Look For—and Look Out For— When Choosing an Advisor?

Not all advisors see retirement planning in the same way—and their mistakes can be expensive, even devastating, for you and your nest egg. Choosing an advisor is analogous to choosing a doctor; that's why you go with a specialist for something as specific as retirement planning, and make sure the person is the right person to meet your needs. Would you go to an OB/GYN to treat your heart condition? Of course not, because cardiologists are much more of an expert in cardiovascular issues. The same holds true for this, especially as you hit the Red Zone and can see retirement on the near horizon.

That said, even among specialists, you'll find a variety of different approaches to retirement planning. As a consumer your aim should be finding the person whose approach aligns best with your stage in life and your goals for the future. Remember that equation we discussed earlier, TR = G + I, or total return equals growth plus income? Keep that in mind as you read the following, because your potential advisor's philosophy regarding what the proper balance is in your specific case and time of life is something you need to understand fully before engaging with them. We've seen too many cases in which a client has been steered to growth-based investments that plainly were not appropriate for where they were in their financial journey. And too often they were surprised to find out how exposed they were, when they'd been assured by their advisor that he or she was.

NATHAN

The reason that most advisors are growth-based is that most of those who are in the industry today got into the business in the '80s and '90s, during what was arguably the strongest stock market in history. We're all the products of our conditioning and our experiences, after all; our beliefs are formed around what we've seen, and what we feel to be true. On some level these advisors believe that being in growth-based stocks is the answer to all investment situations, because in their formative years as financial advisors, that was mostly true. They made those recommendations and looked like rock stars to their clients, who prospered by following their advice. The problem is that those beliefs became set in stone, and these folks can't see beyond those past successes through to the current situation. They've never evolved. And to add to the problem, advisors individually designed their whole business structure around growth-based investments, so not only are they conditioned to adhere to that philosophy, but their companies' existence depends on it.

How can you tell if the advisor you're meeting or working with is one whose approach best matches your needs? Let's talk about some of the approaches and products we often see offered, what we'd see as potential red flags to watch for, and define what we see as a balanced approach.

Red Flag: Cookie Cutter Solutions

You've probably read articles or listened to "experts" touting financial formulas they claim are suited to all cases. However, no single formula is going to work for every unique situation people face. It's a mistake to put too much faith in a financial advisor who offers cookie cutter solutions to retirement planning.

Why do some advisors offer one-size-fits-all solutions?

Well, sometimes the advisors are constrained by the tools their employers offer. They can't offer what they don't have available, so they're stuck with the investment instruments they've got, even if they aren't particularly good ones.

Many advisors rely completely on growth and investment-based portfolios because it's all they really know. They don't understand how to generate income from a portfolio. And while there's nothing wrong per se with growth-based investments, they're not necessarily the best choices when what you're looking for is lower risk, more security, and income from your portfolio. Some financial advisors push products because their employers incentivize them to do so with bonuses, prizes, trips, etc. And while we don't mean to suggest that those who sell them are somehow less than honorable, it's easy to see how, human nature being what it is, some may rationalize selling a client a product as being in both of their best interests when in fact it's not right for that client's needs or time of life.

What do we mean by "cookie cutter plan"?

When you first go to meet with an advisor, they ask you questions regarding your feelings about money, your anticipated needs in retirement, and your assets. That advisor might even run an analysis based on assumptions that are easily manipulated. Having compiled your answers, the advisor hands you what you're assured is a portfolio designed for your specific situation—yet more often than not, that isn't the case.

What we see again and again when we review new clients' existing portfolios is advisors consistently using the same types of mutual funds, bond funds, and ETFs—and typically from the same companies. When we look at a portfolio prepared for a fifty-year-old, and one for a seventy-year-old, and they're effectively the same, something is clearly not right. How could that happen?

"Cookie Cutter"
Portfolio Allocations

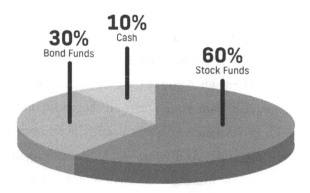

30%
Bond Funds

10%
Cash

60%
Stock Funds

Many of these advisors use automated programs to create port-folios for clients; it's faster and easier for them, but it can and does backfire, because sometimes just putting in the work and doing things the old-fashioned way is the best way. Using these automated programs streamlines the interactions and thus cuts their costs. But the trade-off is that they also lump people into categories. For instance, the program may say that according to your category your portfolio should be 60 percent equities and 40 percent bond funds, or 80 percent equities and 20 percent bond funds. Instead of going out and doing the legwork to find individual positions that generate income that they know these people need, they just follow that guidance and design the portfolio accordingly. That's great from a labor and time management perspective, but it's not always the best thing for the client.

We don't want to believe these are bad people; they aren't nec-essarily doing this intentionally to harm their clients. But it's all they have available to them, or it's just the way they've always done business. As we've discussed, financial advisors come in many varieties, with differing philosophies on investment strategy and with a range of attitudes toward risk. We've noted that at least one firm in our area recommends the same investments so consistently that when one of their clients comes to see us and tells us they're currently using their services, we can tell them what is in their portfolio before they even show it to us! The clients are always surprised at that, but it's not a magic trick. It's just that we've seen so many strikingly similar port-folios coming from this group. While that specific kind of portfolio might be a good fit for some of their clients, it's certainly not suitable for all of them.

We're not suggesting that these advisors are acting in bad faith: They're working with what they have, and, again, their generally more aggressive strategies are right for some people, particularly younger folks who are in the Accumulation stage. But if you're in or closing in on the Red Zone of Retirement, it's time to do things differently.

From our point of view what's often missing in the creation of portfolios is plain common sense. But as grandma used to say, "Common sense isn't so common"—and that applies to financial advising, too.

Our Approach: Your Portfolio Should Be Tailored to You

You are unique; your dreams, your needs in retirement, and your financial situation are specific to you. That's why we typically begin an initial meeting by asking you questions that are designed to help us accurately assess those needs as well as your risk tolerance. What does retirement look like to you? What are the costs you're going to have? What costs will be likely to disappear or be significantly reduced when you retire? What new costs are you likely to have? What's on your wish list? Travel, or a weekend or summer/winter home? Do you enjoy hobbies like golf or boating, and want to spend more time enjoying them?

Your income is critical, so we delve into that: From what sources is your guaranteed income going to be coming: pensions, Social Security, or others? Have you already filed for Social Security benefits, or are you holding off? What will that benefit be when you do file, and when is your optimal age to begin collecting? Will your pension benefits extend throughout your spouse's life as well as your own, or will they be cut or eliminated in the event of your passing?

What are your current spending habits? An accurate accounting of your regular monthly costs and other expenses you incur is required to assess your needs going forward. Remember retirement is all about income, and more importantly the amount of income you are able to keep. So that being said, what do you pay in taxes, and how will retirement be likely to affect that amount?

Do you have a "magic number" in mind? We talked about this in a previous chapter as an example of how having the wrong kinds of goals can actually undermine the effectiveness of your financial planning, and that's certainly true of magic numbers, which can lure you into a false sense of security.

NATHAN

I've got a client who when we first met, told me, "I'm on track." He gave me his 401(k) statement, and it had a neat little pie chart that showed that on the readiness scale, he was above his goal with about $1.1 million in his account. I said, "That's fantastic—but when are you planning on retiring?" He told me that he wanted to retire at sixty-two, which was two years down the road at that point. He explained to me that he and his wife wanted to do some traveling and wanted to enjoy life, so they wanted to retire at an age when that would still be possible; when they'd have their health and the energy and mobility they needed. We started talking about how much income he was going to need in retirement. He told me he was still paying on his house, and that their current income was about $200,000 a year. He didn't want to draw Social Security at sixty-two, but wanted to delay it until he was seventy, if he could. But in running the numbers it became clear that we were going to have to cover about $120,000 worth of income he'd be missing between the ages of sixty-two and seventy with that million bucks he'd saved. Yes, he'd done a great job of saving—but he'd been lulled into thinking that he was in the clear, thanks to that pie chart and his magic number. His goals and dreams for retirement at sixty-two just didn't line up with the financial reality. Fortunately, we were able to get him where he wanted to go by making some adjustments. For one thing, he hadn't been contributing the maximum to his 401(k), so we upped his savings. We set a goal of getting his house paid off, and made a number of other moves toward debt reduction and lowering of expenses that would help him lessen his income needs. I was really glad he'd come in when he did, because he'd have been in for a rude awakening at sixty-two.

At the end of the day, for us this is more than a job. We recognize the responsibility we have to our clients, most of whom stay with us for many years. We don't take shortcuts when it comes to their futures.

Red Flag: Too Many Growth-Based Investments

As we mentioned above, reliance on growth and investment-based portfolios is not a good idea when you are looking for lower risk and more security. Generating true income from your portfolio should be your goal as you approach the Red Zone of Retirement.

LINDSEY

If you're working with a growth-based financial advisor, they're likely to encourage you to take more risks than you really should or need to. Many times the result of being pushed up the risk curve results in the portfolio not producing adequate income needed in retirement. But that kind of investing has been glamorized by the financial services industry, which has done a poor job educating people about the reality of risk and the potential of loss, and the proper ways to generate income. And even though the person advising you may tell you that the funds they're putting you in are very conservative, you need to understand that their definition of conservative and yours could be miles apart. Anyone who's a growth-focused advisor is gambling to some extent with your money, so don't be snowed by their insistence that they're being conservative, because those choices are not at all what a genuinely conservative advisor would make on your behalf.

Our Approach: Bullish on Income

When you're nearing or in retirement, you should be leaning on the I. Our approach begins with determining what amount of income you're going to need, because that's going to determine the type of investments that are best suited for you. Your income needs are likely to increase given inflation and the costs of the goods and services you require. We also factor in things that will impact those numbers, like future healthcare costs.

LINDSEY

Inflation is something that people fail to factor in, thinking it's not going to be as big of a deal as it really is. One way of expressing this impact is to point out that they're going to need three times as much money to cover their regular expenses on their last day of retirement as they did on their first day. We go over the way inflation has historically impacted the costs of everyday expenditures; what did a quart of milk or a head of lettuce cost twenty years ago, compared to its cost today? Rates of inflation can vary, but if you look at inflation over a twenty- or thirty-year time horizon, you can better appreciate how impactful it will be on your savings. People make the mistake of thinking that their cost-of-living adjustments are going to keep up with inflation, but in my experience that has not been the case. Many of these are tied to the consumer price index, which is arguably not all that accurate. And they don't factor in certain costs, like healthcare, that rise when you're retired.

Many people don't have a clear fix on the amount of time that they can hold onto an investment without needing the money. We simply don't like taking unnecessary risks. After all, this isn't a game, and you don't need to run up the score.

First of all, investment accounts are not savings accounts, and you can't treat them as such. Your emergency funds and any money to cover any short-term expenses you're going to have, have to be accessible to you, in a money market account or a savings account—and everyone needs to have an emergency fund. Just because an investment is liquid, you don't want to have to sell it at a loss because you suddenly need the cash when the market is down. We're very clear with our clients about the importance of having emergency funds set aside and readily available—but all we can do is advise.

NATHAN

Sometimes a client will assure us that they have those emergency funds set aside in a savings account, but they'll call us in a panic to say they suddenly need a new car and have to have $20,000 out of an investment account. We talk them through the issues that's going to create for them; how portfolios were set up with clear objectives and goals, and making a big withdrawal is going to impact those objectives. Situations like these underline why it's so important to be open and honest with your advisor about your finances.

When we talk about rebalancing your portfolio, what we're trying to do is mitigate as much risk as possible, and to generate dependable income. If, by investing 80 percent of your portfolio into other kinds of products you can generate enough income to live as you wish in retirement, then the remaining 20 percent can be invested in other ways, and at higher levels of risk if you wish. Your income needs determine your risk tolerance because retirement is all about income. After all, what was your purpose in saving all that money in the first place? In a word, security: the peace of mind that knowing your needs are covered brings. If you're invested in growth-based investments you're taking on risk in exchange for the chance to make money—but it's not genuinely income, because everyone knows the markets don't grow every year and you can't rely on it.

All of this said, what we recommend for each client will be different—and the instruments and investments we recommend need to fulfill each client's unique goals and objectives. The markets and economies will and have always changed. That's why we're not going to go into details here on specific kinds of investments. But when we meet with clients, we're very clear with them about what kinds of options are available, and which we think is best tailored to their needs.

Safety and liquidity are very attractive—but the trade-off and compromise with these investments is that those that offer these advantages have very low rates of return. If you want to increase that rate of return, the trade-off is likely to be a time commitment or risk to the investment. That can be a problem, so it pays to be very clear on what the commitment and compromise really is.

Red Flag: The Advisor Pushes Solutions Without Fully Explaining How They Work

Advisors are in the business of providing investment solutions, but often we find that the solutions offered aren't really explained as clearly as they should be. One of the most often recommended of these is variable annuities. We nearly always find them when we go through a new client's portfolio, but all too often find that the client has no real understanding of how they work. Do you really know what you've got if your portfolio includes them?

Variable annuities are actually just mutual funds with an insurance wrapper around them. Those funds have managers, and they charge fees. The insurance company also adds its fees on top of theirs. These started out years ago as an alternative way to invest in mutual funds and can provide tax deferral. If you invest after-tax dollars within that variable annuity, then you get the benefit of tax-deferred growth. If you don't make withdrawals from the annuity, it grows tax-deferred, but when you do take withdrawals, they're taxable. The idea was that you'd be in a lower tax bracket when that happened, after your working years were behind you and you were in retirement, so you'd pay less in tax.

It began innocently enough, but then these insurance companies started realizing, "Hey, we can start charging fees and promoting these types of contracts," so most of them are commission-based contracts.

Normally the advisor who's selling the variable annuity makes a commission on that product. But when you really do a deep dive into these variable annuities, a lot of them have so many internal fees that it may eat up the benefit of the tax deferral. In most cases you pay to the advisor, and then the insurance company charges a mortality and expense fee. Then, you've got your internal funds, and mutual fund fees, called sub-account fees. Then these insurance companies started tacking on all these riders to the annuities—and charging a rider fee! The variable annuity may have a death benefit rider, or an income benefit rider, or a withdrawal benefit rider attached—all with attending fees. All of these together eat up most of the tax deferral benefit—and you could have invested the same money into a more appropriate investment and avoided all of that.

Some companies sell these as IRAs—which are tax-deferred already, so there's no actual tax benefit to you. To make them more appealing, the insurance companies have started offering you lifetime income benefit features, where they guarantee you a certain amount of income over your lifetime or stated period—but again, there's potentially a fee for that, along with a number of important caveats.

That guaranteed income feature is a bit deceptive, because although you're guaranteed a certain amount of income over your lifetime, that's not based on guaranteed account earnings but based on growth that the account *could* have. And in most cases, should you make any type of withdrawal from your account, it completely negates that year's income benefit increase, because of fees.

While some of them are better than others, none of them are great, because they're a very expensive way to invest. People often don't realize that if the mutual funds within that account don't perform well, they're going to lose, because the fees are so high.

NATHAN

Why would you pay an insurance company for the right to withdraw your own money? It's like going to the bank and saying, "I'm going to put a hundred thousand dollars in this account. And I'm going to pay you 1 percent, or $1,000, for the right to take out my own money in the form of withdrawals."

LINDSEY

If people truly understood how variable annuities work—if all of the fees and conditions attached to them were transparent and disclosed to the client—no one would ever buy one. Because they're associated with insurance companies, people feel secure—"It's safe, I'm insured." But that's not really the case at all.

Our Approach: Client Education

When a new client comes on board, we start by sharing what we know about investing during their allocation meeting, so that they are clear about what their holdings have been, what their options are, and what kinds of investments they should consider going forward, based on their goals, needs, wants, and comfort level. People fall into the habit of letting financial advisors make all the decisions without expecting to really understand the decisions being made. That kind of blind trust isn't smart. We want our clients to understand what their options are, the trade-offs and compromises of each, and help create realistic expectations.

NATHAN

Clients aren't always so thrilled to hear they're expected to be active participants in decision-making. Sometimes they just wave their hands and tell me, "You're the expert, not me! That's why I hired you, to make those decisions." That kind of disconnect is what most of them have been accustomed to, and they're comfortable with it. But we're not. It's not like we expect you to come in knowing everything because for most people, it's not their area of expertise. Even so, we firmly believe that we can do a better job for you if you're a partner in planning. The client's knowledge and that kind of partnership evolves over time. Some people take longer than others to get involved, and that's OK too. But their relief when they do understand where they stand financially is palpable. I compare it to carrying our two-year-old around in this backpack carrier we have. He's a big kid, and he's got a lot of gear—snacks, diapers, bottles—also in the pack. I get used to wearing it, even on a day when it's hot and we're walking a lot, and I forget how much it weighs me down. Then, when I finally take him out of the pack and take it off, it's like a boulder off my shoulders. I hadn't realized how heavy that load was until I was out from under it. I see the same kind of "aha" moment in clients when the mists clear and they understand the concepts we're trying to make clear for them. They didn't realize what a relief understanding their finances would bring until they feel it for themselves.

An example is a lady who came in to see me a few years ago. She was a biology teacher getting ready to retire that year, and a very bright person. The only exposure that she had had to any type of investment advice was through her school district's retirement plan. She laid out her statements for me, and I could see she'd done a very good job of saving, and her Social Security income would be pretty good too, in addition to her pension. Her goal was to spend time with her grandchildren, who were scattered across the country. She dreamed of traveling to Europe and Australia but said she didn't think that was possible for her, because she just didn't have enough money. She knew she'd put together enough to retire on but felt defeated knowing that her other dreams weren't going to come true.

We talked through what she wanted, and I told her, "You're there." She looked at me like I was nuts! So Lindsey and I took her through an allocation meeting, explaining every step of the way in which her money was going to work for her through different investments, making possible these dreams she'd been sure were out of reach. But she was dubious; she'd come in for her six-month reviews, and I'd always ask her if she'd been to visit her grandkids yet. She kept telling me she just wasn't convinced she could afford it. About eighteen months after she became a client, she came in and told me delightedly that she'd taken not one but three trips! She'd finally realized that in fact she could afford it. Her investments were producing true income that she wanted and needed. Her face was just lit up with joy. That weight of worry was off her shoulders at last.

Red Flag: The Advisor Isn't Transparent About Fees and Costs

When people bring their current investment portfolios to us, their challenge invariably is, "Can you do better?" We hear that daily—and just as frequently, we see their shock when we show them the *internal fees* they're paying on those accounts. By and large they have no idea those fees are there.

NATHAN

I'm working with a lady who had watched one of our webinars; she scheduled an appointment to come in and, handing me her portfolio, told me, "I've got this feeling that something's not right. I would like you to do an evaluation and tell me what you find."

I agreed and asked her how long she'd been with her advisor. She said she'd worked with him for twenty years, since she was in her forties, and that she liked him a lot. When I asked her what her advisor was charging her, she told me he wasn't charging her anything. That was odd; obviously the advisor was getting paid somehow, because they wouldn't be in business otherwise.

Examining her portfolio, I saw that most of her funds were what's called Class A, and were front-end loaded funds, meaning there was a 5 percent commission charged to the client when the funds were purchased. Additionally, she was paying an internal fund fee of 1 percent per year—and a 12b-1 on top of that. That's what Lindsey and I would term an egregious fee; it's totally unnecessary, except that it helps cover marketing costs for the funds!

When she came back to meet with me, I shared what I'd discovered with her, and she got very quiet.

I asked her if she was OK, and she said, "This explains everything—because every time I turn around, they're shifting me from one fund into another. When I asked them why, they'd just say, 'That one wasn't meeting your objectives.'" While I didn't think the advisor was churning her funds to make commissions, she was taken aback, and who can blame her?

Keep an eye on the costs of the funds you have, and make sure your advisor explains every fee, every charge and commission, and how they're paid. The better informed you are, the better choices you can make.

Bond funds are not all they are cracked up to be and can open you to risk you might not have been made aware of. The idea behind bond funds is that they're likely to be safer than stocks or equities, and when a person doesn't want or can't afford the risk that stock market exposure creates, owning bond funds is a choice sometimes made by default. But what isn't as widely understood is that when you purchase a bond fund as opposed to purchasing bonds, you're denied the inherent protections that bonds have.

When you own an individual bond, you have a par value that you get back when the bond matures or is called; you have a maturity date, and you have a declared interest rate. That means you know how much interest that bond is going to pay in dollars, as far as interest is concerned, and you have a set maturity date. If you hold that bond to maturity, barring any defaults, you should be able to get the par value back. But when you have a bond fund, you don't own the bond. Effectively, you own stock in a bond-based investment, so those protections aren't there for you.

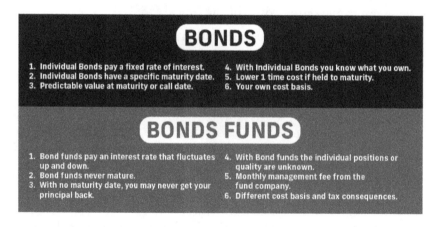

On top of that, bond funds usually have some internal costs and fees associated with them. We find people are paying the advisor who sells them these funds a management fee, or they're paying them a commission to sell them the bond funds—then they're turning around and paying the bond fund company a fee to invest in it! All of these underlying costs can eat up what income the fund is producing, and the elements of risk are why we aren't big fans of bond funds.

That said, there are times when a bond-based electronic traded fund (or EFT) has lower underlying costs, because they aren't commission-based. Buying individual bonds may not make sense at some point because of the price or the interest rate. They don't make sense in every or even most portfolios otherwise, yet we see bond funds in almost every portfolio brought to us for review.

Another investment product that we find many new clients don't fully understand is mutual funds. As with variable annuities, mutual funds are loaded with costs to the client: internal fees and 12b-1 fees, as well as the front-loaded commissions. That said, they still serve a useful purpose, particularly in the portfolios of younger people who haven't hit the Red Zone. It's an easy way for the average young investor without a lot of assets to get into the market, and they do provide a degree of diversification. That's good, and if you're young and investing small amounts per month, you can't effectively diversify your holdings without using ETFs or mutual funds. There are many good funds that keep their investment costs down—but you need to know what those are going in, and your advisor needs to be transparent about that up front, because you don't want your profits eaten up by fees. That said, we prefer to put the effort into choosing individual positions for our clients, so that we can diversify their portfolios while sparing them all the costs and fees mutual funds entail.

The biggest issue with mutual funds from our point of view is that advisors rely on them when their clients are past the point in their lives when the downside risk they pose is no longer appropriate.

All of these instruments have one thing in common: their overuse in portfolios is symptomatic of what we call the Disease of Ease in the financial industry. It's tempting for advisors to rely on them, because they're easy to justify, and they look good to clients who don't understand the fee structures.

Our approach: Full transparency about costs, and multiple options for you

LINDSEY

Again and again what I hear from people coming in to have us check on their portfolios is, "I don't really know what my options are." They've been told at some point, either by their 401(k) managers or their advisors, that their options are limited somehow. They may have started with a 401(k), then moved to a private financial advisor, but the message is the same. They don't share with them the whole universe of options that is out there. We do.

Being offered either/or options by your advisor isn't acceptable; there are always other ways to go, and being told you must choose between a handful of possible investments isn't acceptable. Anyone who tries to tell you that only these specific funds or products are going to work for you is trying to shunt you into a cookie cutter portfolio. Why? Because those are the only instruments available to them—or because they don't want to do the legwork required to do better.

If you've come out of a 401(k) for which you were offered limited choices in investments, you may readily accept that your options continue to be limited. Don't buy it. Just because some advisor's software says you fit into category A, B, or C doesn't mean that the rest of the alphabet is off-limits. Your advisor or the advisor's business structure may be setting those perimeters.

The 401(k)s or qualified plans are many people's initial intro-duction to investments. Within those plans, investment options are generally very limited, and many people find those options so confusing that they turn to their friends at work or their colleague and ask them for advice: "Hey, which of these funds did you pick out of that list?" "Well, I picked this one and that one, and this third one too." The person asking will then just follow his colleague's lead, and opt into the same investments, because frankly trying to make sense of the prospectuses seems like heavy lifting and they don't know who else to ask. The result is usually an inappropriate investment choice for that person.

We focus on investing for the client's goals, needs, objectives, and risk tolerance. If growth-based investments are needed, we attempt to remove as much *unnecessary* risk as possible. There is always some level of risk, even with income-based investments; the question is how to mitigate and lessen the risk. There are many options in the world of non-stock-market income-generating investments. Again, there are no cookie cutter solutions, and what you need won't be the same as what someone else needs. These can vary tremendously, and we delve very deeply into these before choosing among them. We don't go three layers deep; we go five layers deep. It wouldn't be appropriate here to discuss specifically what those investments are because your situation is unique, and it's important to note that all offerings are not created equal. Part of our expertise is knowing their track records, and whether they're appropriate for our clients.

Red Flag: Your Advisor's Definition of "Safe" Could Be Very Different from Yours

If you and your advisor don't share the same definitions of important words, like "risk" and "conservative," you can be lulled into thinking you're in agreement, when in fact your advisor is viewing things through a completely different lens. "Conservative" means one thing to you—but compared to what? The same goes for "risk." Your idea of and tolerance for risk may be very different from your advisor's, and that can cost you your security in retirement.

When you're working with a growth-based advisor, their mindset is already in the aggressive category, because that's where they live. And even though you may tell them you're conservative, in their view that just means less aggressive, not genuinely conservative. That's how people who should be out of risky investments get burned; by not understanding that they just don't see it the way you do. And you may not be entirely clear about where your own views on risk put you, which makes it harder to communicate effectively.

LINDSEY

Even people who know each other well can attach radically different meanings to the same words. I had a married couple in my office the other day who weren't in agreement about what "conservative" should mean as regards their portfolio. Their back-and-forth got so heated I asked them if they'd like me to leave so they could hash it out! The husband didn't want to lose any money on his bottom line—but he wasn't earning enough to keep up with inflation. The wife was OK with losing "a little bit"—but her idea of a little bit was pretty much undefined. Each of them felt that they were the more conservative one in the partnership.

Now, if a couple in a long-term marriage can't agree on what "safe" and "risky" mean, you can see why it's critical to get your advisor to spell out exactly what the risks are with any investment he or she is recommending. If they seem to brush off your questions or suggest that you leave it to them, you're talking to the wrong advisor.

Our approach: Questions and answers

We don't see ourselves as the "bosses" of your investments, but rather as your partners in building you the retirement you deserve. We insist our clients know exactly what they're getting into with every investment: its upsides, its downsides and why we're suggesting it to them at this point in time. That's why we're careful to be clear with them what we mean when we talk about risk versus safety, and to get them to be equally clear with us about their definitions. It's important that in this relationship we nail down not only what we mean with these terms but how they apply to specific investments we recommend.

LINDSEY

A couple had recently become our clients, so we had gotten their account set up and were meeting to go through how and where their money would be allocated. I always start off these meetings by asking people how they'd classify themselves as far as risk tolerance goes. In this case, the husband said, "I feel like I'm an aggressive investor. I like my money to make money, so risk doesn't really bother me." His wife described herself as more moderate in her views, more risk-averse than her husband and not interested in investments that could lose money. When asked how they would have rated themselves before they came to us as clients, they agreed they'd been moderately aggressive.

I took them through the allocation meeting, and we talked about what we deemed conservative versus moderate versus aggressive investments. I spent a significant amount of time explaining examples of each and educating them on the different available options in each group. The funny thing was that by the end of the conversation we all realized the husband was far more moderate in his views than he'd described, and his wife was actually quite conservative.

NATHAN

I have a good friend stationed in the Army at Ft. Campbell in the 101st airborne. Jumping out of an airplane is normal and routine. It's simply part of his job and completely acceptable. He doesn't think about it, stress, or agonize about jumping out of a perfectly good airplane several times a year. He has conditioned and trained himself to accept the risk. I, on the other hand, have done some skydiving in the past and can assure you, there is definitely stress and anxiety involved for me. A person's version of risk is personal and a result of our experiences and environment.

As you can see, so much depends on clear communication between you and your advisor—about fees, commissions, definitions, and options. You need to recognize what your advisor's own mindset is regarding risk, and make sure that they're clear on yours.

But it's important to point out that, in the advisor/client relationship, the communication must flow freely and honestly in both directions. Sometimes the failure to communicate falls on the client, who may not share information they should. That's a bad idea for a lot of reasons, as we'll explain next.

CHAPTER FIVE

What You Don't Know Can Hurt You

Retirement should be a time when you can relax and enjoy the fruits of your labors, secure in the knowledge that your financial needs are being met. "…And they didn't even see it coming" is not a phrase you want applied to your retirement journey. To save yourself and your savings from the unexpected, you've kept a close eye on your investments and your income, and you're feeling secure about your prospects for a comfortable retirement. But there may be some things you haven't considered that could still upend your best-laid plans.

The Challenge: Inflation

Inflation is a big threat that most people underestimate. But it is here to stay, and if you are leaving your savings in savings or other minimal interest-bearing accounts, inflation is sucking the value out of your money. In January 2024, the Consumer Price Index rose 3.1% over the last twelve months, not seasonally adjusted.[1] The cost of goods continues to go up, the costs associated with production go up, salaries rise; it's a naturally occurring cycle. Your fixed costs—your mortgage payment, for instance—won't go up, but everything else does. If your money is earning less than the rate of inflation, you're losing value. And given the low interest rates we're seeing you're losing buying power faster than you should be.

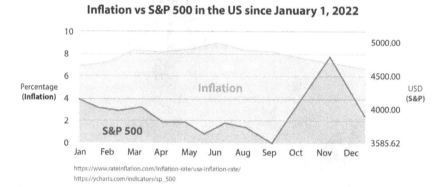

Inflation vs S&P 500 in the US since January 1, 2022

https://www.rateinflation.com/inflation-rate/usa-inflation-rate/
https://ycharts.com/indicators/sp_500

The solution

While inflation presents a moving target, the right kinds of investments can help you to produce enough income to keep up.

The Challenge: Nursing Home Costs

Nobody wants to think about that possibility, but it's a fact that one out of three of us will spend at least some of our retirement in a nursing care facility. Unless you have long-term care insurance, those

---

1   "Consumer Price Index—January 2024," bls.gov, February 13, 2024, chrome-extension://efaidnbmnnnibpcajpcglclefindmkaj/https://www.bls.gov/news.release/pdf/cpi.pdf.

costs are all out of pocket. Even a healthy nest egg could be quickly depleted if you've got nursing home expenses to contend with. To qualify for Medicaid, there's a very limited maximum amount that your spouse will be allowed to keep. As of 2023, spouse can keep $148,620.[2] If your spouse is in good health and has another five or ten years of life ahead of them, that's not going to be enough to see them through. Costs depend on the kind of care you require, and the extras add up. Where you live also has a big impact on pricing. But a millionaire can easily be wiped out, depending on the length of stay.

The solution

A multipronged approach that provides for your needs via several sources of income. Long-term care insurance is one way to address these costs. Back in the '90s is when the concept first gained popularity. But because this was a new product, many insurance companies underpriced it, underestimating what the premiums needed to be to cover the demand. That meant that those premiums had to go up. What happened was that a lot of folks who had paid into those policies for years started seeing their premiums rise just as they hit the age when they were more likely to need nursing home care. Now, they were forced to make serious financial decisions about whether they could afford to keep that coverage they'd been paying into for twenty years or more.

Long-term care insurance is still a good idea—but you must be realistic about what the costs will be, and if they are likely to create a financial hardship given your income. There's no point in paying for a policy that you're going to have to drop later, because you don't have

---

2   "Tennessee: Medicaid Long Term Care Eligibility 2024," seniorplanning.org, January 8, 2024, https://www.seniorplanning.org/long-term-care-medicaid-eligibility/tennessee/.

the income to cover the costs. The best insurance in the world is no good to you if you can't afford it.

There are other ways to cover long-term care costs. You can use investment income, for instance, some type of life insurance or asset-based long-term care plan. Some people choose to set aside a part of their assets to cover any potential long-term care expenses. That way, if they don't use that money, they don't lose it. How you choose to address this depends on your asset level, and how much money is available. In Tennessee, private home healthcare alone may cost an average of $54,000 annually.[3] But if you're in Connecticut or in New York City, you can expect to pay twice that. These kinds of costs are another factor driving the trend to move to areas in which the costs of living are more affordable, and that certainly includes the costs for long-term care.

NATHAN

In my experience, women tend to be more realistic about the need for long-term care, because men assume that they're basically ten feet tall and bulletproof, so they'll never need anything like that. Women are more in touch with reality on that topic. If you talk to a commission-based insurance salesperson about this, they're going to try and sell you a policy, of course. A commission-based financial advisor may advise against you getting that policy, because they want to keep your money in the market. It's important to know that there are better options than either of those choices, and to look at setting them in place before you need them. Putting your head in the sand isn't going to serve you.

---

3   "Nursing Home Costs by State 2023," Wisevoter.com, June 7, 2023, https://wisevoter. com/state-rankings/nursing-home-costs-by-state/#tennessee.

LINDSEY

I've got a client right now who considered his options and decided that he and his wife couldn't afford long-term care insurance. They'd just hope for the best. But his wife now has dementia, so the husband is having to liquidate their investments. When you don't have enough income to cover the cost of care, you have to do what's called a Medicaid spend-down: spending your assets down until you reach the limits required to qualify for Medicaid assistance in covering your care. That's where they are now, and it's devastating.

The Challenge: Devastating Income Loss When a Spouse Passes

Losing your partner is a terrible experience in and of itself—but it can also heavily impact the surviving spouse's income. People still have a lot of misconceptions about Social Security; the surviving spouse doesn't receive two Social Security checks but only the one that's the higher amount. Say the wife's benefit is $2,700 a month, and the husband's benefit is $2,500 a month. If the husband dies in this scenario, the wife keeps her own benefit of $2,700 a month, but she loses $2,500 in household income her husband's check brought in. That's a big change. The problem is exacerbated if people start collecting their Social Security payments earlier than they really should, which also impacts the survivor benefit. What we often hear is, "Well, I might not live that long, so I'd rather start collecting now." But even if you don't live that long, your spouse very well might, and that should be considered before you decide to take your benefits early.

LINDSEY

We see people who have opted to start collecting their benefits at sixty-two, when full retirement age is sixty-seven, taking a 30 percent cut in their monthly benefits for life. I have run benefit analyses for some people for whom that choice makes sense; for instance, someone with a medical condition that will necessarily shorten their life. But for most people, betting against your longevity is a great way to shoot yourself in the foot.

The solution: An in-depth understanding of your benefits coupled with smart income planning

Social Security is so important—and so widely misunderstood—that we put a lot of effort into educating people about how to make those decisions about claiming benefits wisely. We do webinars, seminars, and in-office maximization analyses to help people make better-informed choices.

Pensions vary widely when it comes to survivor benefits. Some people have a 100 percent survivor benefit; some have 50 percent, and some have no survivor benefit at all. Often, as with Social Security, people make bad choices about electing their survivor benefits, in favor of getting more money up front per month. We've talked to many people who opted out of survivor benefits because it was going to cut into their monthly check. That could be bad planning for the support of the surviving spouse. How will they make up that lost income?

NATHAN

The irony is that Americans will spend enormous amounts of money on insurance policies to cover loss of income for the spouse in the event

> of their deaths yet fail to think about their income sources and ways to maximize their income sources that may accomplish essentially the same thing, without the expense of premiums.

In doing these analyses, we look at their primary insurance amount, which is calculated using their work history. We look at their income needs, at their realistic life expectancies, what other income sources they have, and at their taxes. What will the needs of their surviving spouse be? Our software lets us plug in some data and it gives us a comparison analysis that gives people the actual numbers on what they're giving up if they take benefits too early. People try to do those calculations for themselves, but there are a lot of variables they don't take into consideration. It's not as simple as calculating a break-even point. Clearly, if you cannot afford to delay taking your benefit, you must take it, even if it means taking a lesser benefit. But if you have wiggle room, let the wisdom of math be your guide.

The Challenge: Outliving Your Savings

Not realizing how long they're going to live trips up a lot of people when they're planning for their financial needs in retirement. Some people base their expectations on how long their parents or grandparents lived—but actuarial tables tell us that people live longer now than in the past, and that's a trend that is likely to continue. Advances in medicine play a big part in that; open heart surgery used to be a big deal, and now it's practically an outpatient procedure. Too often people sell themselves short on what their realistic life expectancy is.

The solution: Plan ahead for a long life and you can relax and enjoy it

Don't bet against yourself when calculating your needs and the length of time you'll be in the world, because you're risking outliving your money, and that's not a good idea. Your advisor should understand the need for a steady stream of income that will last your lifetime and have ideas on how that can best be provided. When you're guessing about your length of life, this is an area where it pays to be optimistic!

The Challenge: Not Understanding the Impact That Taxes Can Have on Your Retirement Income

…is a common problem. While people are perhaps more aware of this than they were in the past, it's the kind of thing you don't want to learn about too late in the game. Because they're often making financial decisions on the fly, too many people wind up paying more than they need to in income taxes. Sometimes they're making their financial decisions based on their current situation; they took a tax deduction when they invested in their 401(k), rather than opting for a Roth IRA, which could be a better choice.

The solution: Remember—retirement is about income, and proper planning can't just be about the here and now

Granted, tax laws change all the time, but you need to look down the road when you're planning and set up your retirement accounts to protect you from paying more taxes than you should. That may mean contributing to a Roth IRA rather than to a pre-tax 401(k), for instance. It can also mean using tax-advantaged investments wisely in retirement, rather than putting your money into taxable investment funds as you did when you were younger.

LINDSEY

I had a conversation with a lady recently; she's sixty-six, and her husband is sixty-eight and they're fully retired now. She handles the investments in their household, and she just learned this year that when they turn seventy-three they've got to start taking $60,000 a year out of their retirement plans. They hadn't figured out the required withdrawal from their investments prior to the time they needed to remove them, so she's rushing around trying to figure out how to do Roth conversions. Their planning had this flaw in it, all because they didn't understand the ramifications of the tax laws on their retirement savings. If she'd had more time, she could have made better choices.

The Challenge: Assuming You'll Be in a Lower Tax Bracket

Assuming you'll be in a lower tax bracket when you retire is another widely held misconception. Surprisingly, many people suddenly find themselves in a higher tax bracket when they retire, especially when those minimum distribution requirements kick in at seventy-three. Sure, they saved money at the time they invested in those pre-tax accounts—but now the bill is coming due. Saving on taxes was the incentive, but they're finding that they're either not saving on taxes or it's not nearly the level of savings that they thought it would be.

The solution: Consider relocating to a state with lower or no taxes

To some extent the problem is mitigated (or exacerbated) by where you live, at least as far as state taxes are concerned. Several states don't have state income tax. We know that states that don't have state income tax usually have higher sales tax rates, but where you retire can have a huge impact on your retirement success. Cost of living should be another part of your retirement planning, if possible.

The Challenge: Hanging onto Investments

Hanging onto investments that might have been good at one point but are no longer paying off is a common problem. Sometimes that's a result of what we call "emotional investing," which we'll talk more about in the next chapter. Often the problem is that they have used market investments for so long that they're stubbornly convinced that those investments will continue to bear fruit.

The solution: Expect the inevitable downturn, and plan accordingly

Downturns happen, as we've seen many times over the years, and if you're at the stage in life where a market downturn could impact your retirement plans, you need to be realistic about the purpose of the money. The investments you own need to match your investment objectives, as well as your current stage of life. Your money will serve its purpose, and you'll sleep better at night.

The Challenge: Your Financial Experts Don't Communicate with Each Other

We talked about this earlier, but it bears repeating. If your tax accountant, your attorney, and your investment advisor aren't aware of changes in your income, your marital status, your needs, your health, or anything that may impact your financial situation—they need to be.

The solution: Get them acquainted and on the same page

This is on you; if your financial people aren't all connected in some way already, you need to take an active role in getting them in touch with each other and aware of each other's planning regarding your retirement. People at some point realize that their financial planning, their tax planning, and their estate planning are generally related to one another. Make sure those communication lines are open, and that all hands know what the others are doing. We're only as good as the information we have to work with, and even the best in the profession can't read minds. Work with your experts and they'll do a better job for you.

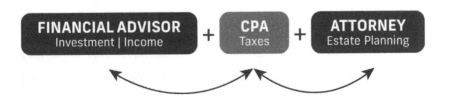

How Can You Keep These Kinds of Challenges from Cropping Up?

When you hit the Red Zone of Retirement, that five-to-ten-year point ahead of your retirement, that's the time to sit down, look at all these factors, and plan for those minimum distributions. Just because you're retired doesn't mean you won't owe taxes on any passive income you've still got coming in, though a surprising number of people don't think about that. This is the point in your life when proper planning can make the difference between a retirement of ease or a retirement of worry, and the closer you get to taking those minimum distributions, the less options you'll have in planning for them. Start looking at those options now, not later, to try to reduce your tax liability down the road and get rid of unnecessary risk.

- *Make sure your assets are allocated properly for the distribution phase.* This goes back to the tools that are appropriate in the accumulation stage, which can backfire drastically in the distribution phase.

- *Know how much income your investments are actually generating, and what could impact that figure.* A lot of people don't understand their investment statements, or don't read them closely enough to understand the various fees they're paying. They don't consider that a market downturn could force them to sell shares and cut into their principal. Those forced withdrawals also impact their income taxes, because they have to be reported as income. There is a difference between income planning and having investments that actually generate income.

- *If your investments are needed for income in any form, they should be producing at least that level of income.* That doesn't mean that you're not going to get growth on the investments. It just means that they should be balanced properly, allocated in a way where you're not spending more money than you're making. If your investments aren't earning what you've got to take out in income, you're spending more than you're making. If you spend more than you make, as a general rule, you run the risk of running out of money.

- *Are your investments allocated appropriately* for when you start taking your required distributions? You need to look and see how much income your investments are generating. It's just common sense, but a lot of very intelligent people don't see it until it's explained to them. Once again, don't be fooled by firms using the term *income planning*. There is a difference between income planning and investments that actually generate income. Income planning may just be fancy terminology for spending down principal, and maybe you won't run out of money before you run out of life.

- *Remember that tax planning is an ongoing process, not a one and done.* The laws change all the time, and you must readjust your financial strategies to make up for that. Don't rely on your tax accountant to do this for you. Your advisor should be able to help you with an efficient tax plan that works with your investments. If you don't keep up with changes in tax law, you may find yourself scrambling to shore up your financial security late in the game.

To help our clients avoid these pitfalls, we strive to make sure everything's done in coordination with experts with whom we work, tax planners and tax preparation services, and estate planning. You need to be sure you're doing the same.

CHAPTER SIX

"What Is the Purpose of This Money?"

The answer to the question above may seem so obvious that you can't understand why we'd bother to pose it. But if you don't ask yourself this question every now and then, you can wander offtrack in how you plan for retirement. Understanding what you're aiming for and what's driving your choices in terms of how you grow and protect your money is mission critical to success, regardless of your answer.

Maybe your purpose is a big one-time purchase, something you've dreamed of, like a yacht, or a cabin on a lake somewhere. Maybe it's a luxury trip around the world, with plenty of time to explore. Or your dream might be leaving a legacy to your family, or some cause you're passionate about, and that's your "why." It could be that you simply want to live a comfortable, adventurous retirement with plenty of income and no worries about money. It could be some combination of these. Whatever it is, it's very important that your investment strategy align with the purpose of the money.

If you're investing money for a purpose, your investments need to be able to meet that purpose. If for instance you're looking ahead to a big lump sum purchase, you may need to continue to invest for capital appreciation, so that in the equation $TR = I + G$, you'd be going for growth.

But if the purpose of the money is to provide a legacy for your family, or to provide income for the rest of your life, your investments need to align with that. You'll need to focus more on what kind of income your money is producing for you. How much in interest and dividends have you got coming in?

When we ask this question in our adult education seminars, the vast majority of the people tell us that their purpose is to secure a comfortable lifestyle and dependable income that will support them throughout retirement. But what we also find is that often their investment style runs counter to that goal—can in fact blow it up—because they haven't properly connected it to their goal.

Does Your Investment Style Match Up with Your Purpose?

The people we work with have all kinds of investment styles and preferences. Some describe themselves as risk-takers, while others embrace a more conservative approach. Many people tell us that they're risk-averse and are shocked when we point out components of their existing portfolios that are anything *but* conservative. That discrepancy between what kinds of investments they think they hold and what they actually have usually boils down to the difference between how their advisor defines "conservative" and how the client would define it, which can lead to all kinds of misunderstandings and misallocation of funds. There are times in our lives when either an aggressive or conservative approach, or a combination of the two, is most appropriate, and we've discussed those stages in investment life in previous chapters. And as noted above, our purpose—our ultimate goal, whether that be a big one-time dream-come-true purchase or a comfortable retirement without stress—should dictate our strategy. This makes logical sense, and that's how we should approach our retirement planning. Knowledge is power, and the more you know about where you are and how your money is working for you, the more power you have.

But there's another kind of investor whose choices aren't really based on knowledge, reason, logic, or strategic thinking, and those folks are very often what we call *emotional investors*. While many peoples' investment strategies include a component of emotion, making financial choices chiefly or sheerly based on feelings is a bad, bad idea.

What Is an Emotional Investment?

Here's an example. We worked with a client whose whole career had been spent working for one company, and his 401(k) was mostly invested in that company's stock. He was fine with that; he loved his former employer and believed in the service they provided. They had taken good care of him, he felt, and so he owed them his loyalty. The stock wasn't performing particularly well, though it had been higher in the past, and he told us he'd decided that if it hit that high benchmark again, he'd consider selling it. He'd retired at this point and really didn't want to sell, he admitted, because he felt on some level it was disloyal.

That was an emotional investment that wound up hurting him, because in fact the stock tanked, dropping about 40 percent—and taking a good piece of his retirement account with it. Clearly, if he'd been thinking with his head rather than his heart, he'd have been better off.

Sometimes, it's a family affair...

It isn't always the case that the emotional investor is stuck on a stock because they worked for the company. Another client we met with was emotionally attached to a stock because his father had held those shares until he'd passed away and had willed his shares to his son. When we questioned whether this stock was really the best investment for him at that point in his life, he told us he still believed in the stock, that it had done well for his father, and that he had a sentimental attachment to it. He would not be parted from it.

In a third instance, a client had stock in a bank that his grandmother, an immigrant, had invested her savings in when she first came to this country. The bank was started by someone who was from the same area she'd grown up in, and so that stock had a double meaning, not only as a gift from a beloved grandmother but also as a piece of the family's ethnic heritage. Now this third-generation stockholder could see that the stock wasn't doing well, but although he was clear-eyed about his other investments, he had held onto this one far longer than he should have.

...But what would dad really have wanted you to do?

Typically, what we say to people with this kind of emotional attachment to an investment is, would your family member have held onto that stock if it had been underperforming or losing value? Would they have wanted you to lose the money you had in the stock when it was performing poorly? Looking at it in this way often helps them to make the separation between what the stock represents to them—love, a parent's gift, heritage, or family loyalty—versus its real value to them today in financial terms. The problem is that they view what should be a strictly financial question as though it was an heirloom, rather than what it really is, and worry that it's a kind of betrayal if they get rid of it. But what the parent or grandparent probably wanted to leave them was a source of financial security, not an obligation.

Nearly All Investments Have Some Emotional Component to Them

If you invest or hold onto investments solely because of your feelings about them, that's very foolish. Smarter choices are made when emotional choices are tempered by logic and facts. Yes, an investment should "feel" right. But that shouldn't be your primary reason for making or holding onto an investment. What you do with your money has to make sense for you in your specific situation. Inherited investment strategies may not be the best choice for you.

Often, we see people holding onto investments that were left to them by family members because they simply don't know what to do with them; they aren't comfortable in the financial realm, and they're afraid to make a change. What if they choose wrong, and lose the money their parents worked so hard to give them? That's another kind of emotional investing—being rendered passive by fear of making a mistake—that can also cost you. Just letting something ride because you're afraid that you'll do the wrong thing isn't a smart way to go. Better to educate yourself and see what's out there, so you can make choices that are smart for you.

When we ask people why they hold onto investments like this, they'll often say it's not really for any specific reason. But in our view, there's a reason behind every choice we make in life, so we probe a little more deeply and encourage them to look for their reason. If it's something along the lines of, "My parents just liked it and thought it was a good investment," we can talk about that. Is it currently a good investment? Are they making money on it, or losing money on it? How secure is their money in that investment, and how badly would losing that money impact their security going forward? What is their ultimate goal with that investment? Do they want to pass the investment onto their children? What if the investment passes on to your children—will they benefit from it? When we're talking with emotional investors, we often take them through stock market history to illustrate our reasoning, because the stock market's history has a distinct cycle that reliably repeats itself, and downturns are part of that. Can they afford to have a significant part of their personal wealth at risk in a downturn? Do they have the time to make up for those lost investments?

LINDSEY

There are also what's called Black Swan events—unpredictable, out-of-left-field events that impact markets across the world, like the COVID-19 virus. These events can set off market downturns that take years to correct.

If it's stock we're talking about, and their ultimate goal is to pass it on to their children, what's the realistic time horizon as far as their kids are concerned? Will they also feel too attached to it to liquidate it, and wind up holding onto it longer than they should? If so, they could be subjecting themselves to whatever happens with the natural cycle of the stock market as well. I find that's something that a lot of people really haven't thought about. When you get them thinking about it, they very often realize that, "yeah, they are probably going to sell this as soon as I'm gone." Honestly, it depends on what the heirs' ultimate time horizon looks like as well. Once you get people to see this and acknowledge it, they begin to understand the importance of separating emotions from their investments.

NATHAN

I had a highly intelligent, very sweet lady coming to the office about a year ago. This is a very common situation; her husband had been the one who managed their finances and made their investments, and now he had passed away about five years prior. She was the one who took care of the household budget and monitored their savings.

She confessed she hadn't paid much attention to the investment decisions, but told me, "I've done all the budgeting. I've lost a sizable amount of my income because my husband passed. I want you to look at this portfolio because I've got this feeling in the back of my mind that I'm holding on to this for the wrong reason, because my husband set it up." It's rare to have people show that degree of self-awareness about an emotional attachment, but she badly needed income, because her income had been cut in half.

She was squeaking by, but just barely, she admitted, and said, "I'm worried that our investments are not set up the way I need them to be set up now." It may have been perfectly fine before her husband passed because they didn't need that money to generate income. They had plenty of income. After I looked at their portfolio, I found that she was right. Her portfolio was generating very little income. Fortunately, we were able to help her.

Would that lady's late spouse have been happy that his wife was reduced to living on the edge because of her loss of income? Of course not! His intention in building an investment portfolio was to guarantee their financial stability. But what had perhaps been suitable investments when they were both living were no longer suitable when she was on her own. That's why it's important to reevaluate your portfolio whenever you have a significant change in your life, and rebalance it as needed. Sometimes the money can safely be left where it is, but often some adjustments need to be made, and emotions, as painful as they are, shouldn't stand in the way.

Other Ways Emotion Can Drive Your Financial Choices

There are other kinds of emotional investing we see, unrelated to family sentiment or corporate loyalty. Some people are addicted to speculation, the riskier the better. For the thrill-seeking, the excitement of taking a financial risk generates a powerful adrenaline fix that creates excitement—and excitement is certainly a compelling emotion. These same people would probably take offense if you were to point out that they're not very far away from dumping their life savings on the craps table in Las Vegas, as far as taking potentially ruinous risks with their security is concerned. But that's what they're doing, and many of them can't be reasoned out of it.

People can also be gripped by negative emotions that cause them to make poor choices. Fear is a big one. These days, the network news is enough to terrify anyone; the sky is falling, the market is about to crash, the federal reserve is going to take us back to the gold standard, etc., etc. The fearmongering is across the media, and it's very effective in a negative way. On the other side, you see professional media pundits who act as stock market cheerleaders, and who believe against all odds that the market can't go anywhere but up. Sometimes this kind of blind optimism comes from being too young to have gone through a downturn, or may be just a function of natural youthful ebullience. We saw an article the other day that said 59 percent of Gen Z investors confessed to drunk trading, as did 9 percent of baby boomers, and overall, 32 percent... not exactly a ringing endorsement of their financial judgment![4] Why do they think casinos serve free alcohol to people at the gambling tables? It's not because they want you to have fun. It's because they know that if you're impaired in any way, that's going to cloud your judgment and you're more likely to engage in risky behavior.

Another kind of emotional investment is the belief that what was a successful choice for someone in the past is bound to succeed for them again. This can work sometimes, but too often it's the equivalent of expecting lightning to strike twice in the same spot. You made money in precious metals back in '11? That's great, but that doesn't mean you're going to see that kind of rise again, because the pressures on the markets are different from what they were then. That said, we do believe that there are time-tested investments that are more reliable than others when it comes to holding or growing value. But just because something worked well in the past doesn't necessarily mean it will work for you again. Even less does it mean you should put all of your eggs in that particular basket.

---

4   Weston Blasi, "Amid 'gamification' Concerns, Nearly 6 in 10 Gen Z Investors Admit to Trading While Drunk," MarketWatch. com, August 19, 2021, https://www.marketwatch.com/story/ more-than-half-of-gen-z-investors-admit-to-trading-while-drunk-11629382517.

We talked above about how losing a loved one can cause people to hang onto investments that may no longer really serve them, because of sentiment attached to the person who made those investments. But there's another kind of emotional response to a loss that can be equally damaging. When you're still in the grip of grief is not the time to be making any kind of major, potentially life-altering choices. When we meet with recently widowed people, our advice is to make no important decisions for a year at least. People do all kinds of things in this state that they regret later. They sell their homes, or liquidate their assets, get rid of things they should have held, and so forth. That first year is the hot zone, when emotions are still too raw and overwhelming to allow you to see things clearly. Don't rush into or out of anything when you're in this situation. Most things can wait—and should wait—until you're emotionally equipped to face them.

LINDSEY

We've seen people who are just too scared to make any kind of decision regarding their investments, because they're so afraid they'll choose badly. They don't really trust themselves or anyone else, so they wind up leaving too much of their nest eggs in CDs or bank accounts, because that's their comfort zone. In my observations, this happens because nobody has ever really taken the time to educate them about their options. That's one extreme; the other is those people who are stubbornly aggressive in their investments, even when that isn't sensible, given their stage of life. Being too extreme in either direction can break your retirement nest egg.

Is This Ringing a Bell for You?

If you're reading this chapter and recognize that on some level you are an emotional investor, now is a good time to ask yourself some questions. First, when your family member gifted you with these investments, what do you think was their intention about the ultimate gift? Was it really the investments? Or were the investments just the vehicle by which they hoped to increase your worth and security? That's what investments are—money in another form, not an heirloom. Would they have wanted you to lose that worth and security, or would they have wanted you to be a good steward of the money?

If your emotional attachment to an investment is too great, you may agree with everything we say here, but still not be able to part with it. We've seen it happen; our client described above, the fellow who was left the investment by his father, realized that his attachment wasn't logical or even sensible, but chose to hang onto the failing investment regardless, because he was so certain that it was what his father would have wanted him to do. We disagreed on that choice, but it was his choice, and having made our reasons for differing clear, we had done all we could. He would not be moved. That happens more often than we'd like.

Your Advisor Can Help!

As investment advisors, our job is to be the voice of reason that helps the client get clear about the emotional component attached to an investment and help them to view it from a more logical perspective. That can be difficult with new clients because there needs to be a level of trust built up in the relationship before the client is open to hearing what we have to say, and accepting that we're urging them to act in their own best interests, rather than in service to some hidden agenda on our parts. But we are very often able to help people, as tough as it is. We don't push; we don't ignore the power of the emotions driving their choices. We just try to illuminate the situation and guide them toward more thoughtful and appropriate choices.

And Make Sure Your Spouse Is Informed, and on Board

If you are the person in your marriage who handles the financial end of things, please don't leave your spouse in the dark regarding your investments—even if that's where they'd rather be. Make sure they are aware of the purpose of the money, where the money is, why it's where it is, and what they have to do should anything happen to you. Develop a relationship with an investment advisor whom you can trust, and take your spouse with you to your meetings with that person. Make sure they attend your portfolio reviews, too, and understand what they're hearing. You've probably put a good deal of thought and time into your investments with the aim of ensuring you and your spouse's safe financial future. But all that work can be undone if your grieving spouse makes ill-informed or rash decisions when you're gone. Make your spouse your real partner when it comes to your money, and you can rest easier knowing that they're equipped to look after themselves if you're gone.

Bottom Line

Being in touch with our feelings is a good thing—but when it comes to investments, we need to lead with our heads, not our hearts. Even if a particular asset was a good choice for your parent or grandparent, or performed for you well in the past, it may not represent the best use of your money today. That's why it's important to work with an advisor you trust.

As we've said before, no portfolio is a "set it and forget it" proposition. No investment is guaranteed to be profitable in the future just because it was profitable in the past. Good advisors understand that circumstances change, markets change, and what worked well for someone at an earlier stage of their investment lives probably isn't the best choice for that person when they reach retirement. And just as situations change, management changes in companies and in fund groups. If your dad was your advisor in your youth and told you then that a specific group of mutual funds was the best, that might no longer be the case. You still need to reevaluate your holdings on a regular basis, and a good advisor will help you by helping you see where your feelings about a holding may be at odds with what's really best for you now.

CHAPTER SEVEN

Common-Sense Investing

The common-sense approach we take to our work informs the tools we use to help our clients generate the income they need going forward. People are invested in their advisors, in a sense; they've often been with the same person for years but come to us because they're increasingly concerned about market fluctuation or the inability to produce enough investment income. Some folks haven't actually worked with an advisor in the past, but come to us with 401(k)s in which the risk was baked in, if you will, by what funds the manager invested in. That's a forced level of risk, and now they're wondering if that's where they should remain.

NATHAN

I think many people truly don't realize that they have a voice when it comes to expressing how comfortable they are or not. I really believe that people are often quite uncomfortable with the risk they're taking, yet they accept it because they don't realize they have a choice. And if they do think they have a choice, I believe that a lot of times they feel that their only alternative is not getting any return on their money at all—as though the choice is between staying where they are or just pulling out altogether and putting their nest egg under the mattress, into the bank, or into low-paying CDs. They've been forced to make the best of an uncomfortable situation because they don't see the alternatives, and their advisor doesn't tell them about them. Let the wisdom of math be your guide.

"Why do I need to generate income from my investments?" is a question we hear from new clients fairly often. The answer lies in history—specifically, the history of the stock market's cyclic, regular swings from bearish to bullish, which has to be part of any savvy investor's planning process. Without a grasp on the history of the market, you're liable to put yourself and your savings at risk.

Suzy came to see us for the first time in 2013. Clearly agitated, she explained that she and her husband Charlie had retired in 1998. Charlie was great at investing, and they had a financial advisor who had told them, "You guys are in great shape. You've got a million dollars in your 401(k), so we'll roll it over into an IRA. What do you want from this account?" Her husband had said if they could take $40,000 a year from it, they could live their dream retirement. The advisor pointed out that the account had been averaging a return of almost 8 percent, so them taking just 4 percent or $40,000 a year should be very doable. He kept them in a growth-based investment strategy.

About a year later, Suzy said, Charlie was in a catastrophic car accident that he didn't survive.

Charlie had always been the one who dealt with the financial advisor, but now Suzy had to go see him alone. He reassured her that everything was fine; their portfolio was averaging nearly 9 percent a year, so she could continue to pull out the $40,000 a year as before.

But in 2000, the dot com bubble burst, and 9/11 wasn't far behind. The market tanked, going down 40 percent, though it recovered in 2007. All the while Suzy continued taking out the $40,000 a year. Then, in 2008, we had the housing default crisis, with all the credit default swaps, and the stock market went down almost 50 percent. Still, Suzy continued to take out $40,000 a year.

Then in 2013, one day she opens up her statements and sees that where they'd started out with a million dollars, now she was down to $514,000. She panicked; just a few days before her doctor had examined her and told her he was confident that her excellent health meant she could easily live into her nineties. She'd come to me, wanting to know how this could have happened.

The reason was very simple. When they retired, their advisor failed to adjust their investment strategy to meet the purpose of the money, which was to provide Charlie and Suzy with an adequate income stream so that they could live the retirement of their dreams.

In the years when the market was down, Suzy had to sell more shares to get her $40,000 out. The years the market was up, she had to sell fewer shares. But one way or the other, she was still selling shares—and shares represent principal.

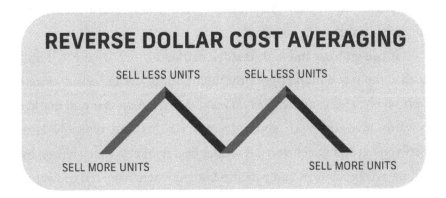

REVERSE DOLLAR COST AVERAGING

SELL LESS UNITS   SELL LESS UNITS

SELL MORE UNITS   SELL MORE UNITS

When you retire, the sequence of returns becomes critical. If there's a market downturn for a few years, after you've retired, it's almost mathematically impossible to recover. Of course, the market might go up—but history shows us that it won't keep going up indefinitely, and those downturns can crush your nest egg. If, like Charlie and Suzy's advisor, you focus solely on growth and capital appreciation, sequence of returns can break you.

This takes us back to the first principle: TR = G + I and knowing what the purpose of your money is. If it's intended to provide you with a stable and comfortable income in retirement, then your investment strategy needs to match your investment objectives. And you can't count on the market to come through for you. If the purpose of the money is to provide income, you can invest for income by investing for interest in dividends. These have lower risk; you can stay in the market using a dividend strategy, which means you're not giving up on growth and capital appreciation.

A Brief History of the Stock Market

Generally speaking, do you believe that history repeats itself more often than not? We certainly do. When we meet people nearing retirement whose portfolios are heavily invested in the market, we take the time to explain why understanding market history is critical to their financial health going forward.

If you go back and look at stock market history, what you'll find is that the stock market goes through natural cycles, called *secular bear market cycles* and *secular bull market cycles*. A secular bull market rewards investors with above-average returns and typically lasts between ten and fifteen years. A secular bear market is characterized by below-average returns and will also last anywhere from ten to twenty years. There may be rallies within secular bear markets where stocks or indexes rise for a period, but the gains are not sustained, and prices then sink to lower levels.

Given that kind of timeline, what are the chances of a person retiring and living their full retirement career in a secular bull market cycle, with its ever-higher returns? Alternately, what are the odds of an unfortunate person retiring at the very beginning of a secular bear market cycle, which simply means that the market is not going to see any growth and possibly steep losses during that time? Those are the two extremes, but it's probably more likely that in retirement an investor will be drawing money from retirement accounts in a period that includes both kinds of cycles. This is why it's critical that investors understand how the cycles work and how to plan and invest for them.

Without diving into a deep pool of analytical data, it's instructive to go back and look at what's happened in the market over one hundred or so years. From around 1900 to 1921, the stock market was in a secular bear market cycle.[5] A disciplined growth-based investor who was not taking any withdrawals from their investments during that time saw zero growth. During that period of time, there were years where the market did better than others, but from around 1900 to 1921, it was a zero-sum game.

That changed in 1921–1929 when the stock market hit a secular bull cycle with its exponential upswing in investments.[6] That meant your disciplined buy and hold investor enjoyed tremendous growth in their portfolio. That all fell off the cliff in the market crash of 1929, where millions lost everything they had in the longest and deepest downturn in our nation's history. What became known as the Great Depression lasted over a decade, until the beginning of World War II

5   https://stockcharts.com/

6   https://stockcharts.com/

in 1941. From 1929 to about 1954, there were periods of time when the stock market did well, some years better than others. But once again, your disciplined buy and hold investor who was not taking any money from their accounts during that period of time saw a 0 percent return of growth—again a zero-sum game.

The postwar years led to a new bull market from about 1954 to 1966, and investors realized a huge amount of growth. But 1966–1982 saw the return of the secular bear market cycle. Your disciplined buy and hold investor realized no growth during that period of time, basically ending up where they'd started.

The cycle from 1982 to the year 2000 was arguably the best bull market run in history. Your disciplined buy and hold investor who was invested during this period of time saw substantial growth.

When investors in the bull market got used to all this growth and capital appreciation in their retirement portfolios, they were probably thinking it would never end. But what happened in the year 2000? It got ugly; when we look at the S&P 500 from the years between 2000 and 2002, the stock market lost 40 percent of its value. It took a little bit over two years to find the bottom. Between 2002 and 2007, it recovered 100 percent of what it lost. It took the S&P 500 until 2007 to regain the ground it had lost since 2000. New investors got brave and got into the market as the real estate bubble swelled.

Then, in 2008, the stock market lost 50 percent of its value, and this time, it took only a little more than a year to hit bottom. Between 2008 and 2013, it recovered 100 percent of what it lost; in 2013, it crept back up to where it was in 2007 and also where it was in the year 2000. Our disciplined buy/hold investor who was withdrawing no money from their portfolio during that period of time was rewarded with zero growth. [7]

---

7   https://stockcharts.com/

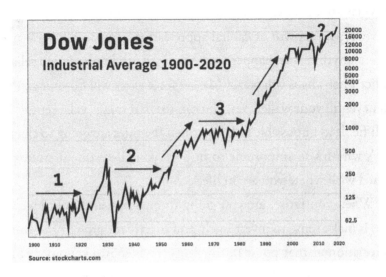

Source: stockcharts.com

Why is this important? We want you to understand that averages can be deceiving. Now, during long periods of time of stock market history, you might look back and see the S&P 500 average during a period of time—twenty years, thirty years, forty years, sixty years—and you might find figures there of 6 percent average per year, 7 percent or 8 percent average per year—whatever it might happen to be because it changes depending on what's going on with the markets. But let's give it the benefit of the doubt and let's say that the S&P 500 is averaging an 8 percent return. Once again, those averages can be very deceiving. Let me give you an example: What if I were to tell you that Lindsey and I run an average of ten miles per week? Your immediate assumption would probably be, "Wow, they must be pretty fit, because that's a lot of running every week." But what if I tell you that I didn't run at all—that it was Lindsey running twenty miles a week on her own? You can see how the "average" suggests a different story than the true one.

Let's put this in perspective where your financial health is concerned. In those years in which the stock market has a lot of growth and capital appreciation, you're obviously better off financially.

But what about those bear market cycles, when it's a zero-sum game and there's no growth or capital appreciation? To paraphrase Warren Buffett, anything can happen in the markets, and nobody can reliably predict when chaos will occur. Market forecasters will fill your ears but will never fill your wallet. Yes, you can see that these cycles repeat, but it's difficult to impossible to know when the tides are going to change. That's why it's so important to be sure your investment strategy is aligned with where you are in life.

When you retire, are you going to be a buy and hold investor? Does it make sense to invest solely and strictly for growth and capital appreciation at that point in time in your life? Are you going to be making withdrawals from those investments? During those times of secular bear market cycles, when there's no growth realized, you may end up having to take money out of principal. You are selling shares with the hope that the shares grow in value. The key word is hope.

When it comes to the stock market, history does have a tendency to repeat itself—so why don't we all automatically adjust our investment strategies to align with where we are in life? Wouldn't it make sense to reduce risk at a point in life where we can't afford the downside? Doesn't it make sense to have the purpose of the money match the objective of the investment? Clearly—but many people just can't let go, even though common sense and the wisdom of math would seem to dictate a different investment strategy if we don't have time to wait for a new bull market.

Why is this? I believe it has to do with human nature. The famed money manager, Sir John Templeton, once said, "The four most expensive words in the English language are, 'This time it's different.'" We're all guilty of that kind of magical thinking at some point in our lives, and we've all paid varying prices for the mistakes that thinking has led us into. When you're riding high in a bull market, it's dangerously easy to be seduced into thinking it will last forever—in other words, this time it's different. But it's not—not if you look at the history.

Now, I'm not trying to broadcast doom and gloom, or suggest that the sky is falling and everything is going to come to an end. But understanding and learning from history may prevent you from making the same mistakes that others have made in the past. If we don't learn from those mistakes, we're doomed to repeat them. That's why understanding these secular market cycles is critical, along with understanding where you are in the Life Cycle of Investing. If you're withdrawing money from these investments in any form in a downturn, relying on growth and capital appreciation could be very detrimental to your overall plan.

Imagine the pain of those who retired in 1999, then watched their nest eggs shrivel through successive secular bear cycles. They'd gotten used to what looked like limitless growth and capital appreciation. They may have advisors who got in business during that time, so that all they'd ever known was a bullish stock market. They taught people how to invest for growth and capital appreciation, which is a good way to go if you're thirty or forty years of age. But there's a point at which it's wise to pull back from the market and seek out safer investments, and if you didn't do that as a retiree in that period, you lost a lot.

That's what we're talking about here: adjusting your investment strategy to make sure you're earning enough in dividends and interest to satisfy what you're having to pull out. It's really very simple: making sure you're earning enough in dividends and interest on accounts that you know you're going to have to make withdrawals from. That doesn't mean if you have a Roth account or after-tax account that maybe you're not taking any withdrawals from that account. You have no plans on taking withdrawals from that account at all. Does that mean that you can't invest that account for capital appreciation?

Absolutely not. That doesn't mean there's some magic bullet or a single product that's the answer for everyone—but it's critical to your financial health that you know alternatives that might be right for you.

Let's Talk About Income

When we meet with new clients the first time, we spend that meeting assessing their financial fitness, both now and going forward in-depth to learn about their goals for retirement and to accurately assess whether they're on track to hit them.

Some of the areas we explore are these: From what sources is your guaranteed income going to be coming: pensions, Social Security, or others? Have you already filed for Social Security benefits, or are you holding off? What will that benefit be when you do file, and when is your optimal age to begin collecting? Will your pension benefits extend throughout your spouse's life as well as your own, or will they be cut or eliminated in the event of your passing?

What are your current spending habits? An accurate accounting of your regular monthly costs and other expenses you incur is required to assess your needs going forward. What do you pay in taxes, and how will retirement be likely to affect that amount?

Do you have a "magic number" in mind? We talked about this in a previous chapter as an example of how having the wrong kinds of goals can actually undermine the effectiveness of your financial planning, and that's certainly true of magic numbers, which can lure people into a false sense of security.

We introduce our clients to dollar cost averaging. When you're consistently investing money in the stock market, you're buying high and you're buying low and you're averaging out your share price. Over time, as the market goes up, if you have a lower average share price, you can sell those shares for a profit. You can increase your return using dividends, because if your investments are paying dividends and you don't need those dividends for income, they're constantly buying new shares, so you're continuing to dollar cost average using your dividends. This is a very powerful strategy. Think about it, you are no longer employed with earned employment income but you can still dollar cost average with dividends increasing your total return and consistently building your income for future use.

Most importantly we walk you through alternatives to the risks built into your portfolio and explore options that may be safer and more reliably productive for you. At the end of the day, it's about peace of mind—and protecting yourself from the inevitable market swings. That, to us, is just common sense.

Bottom Line

What was right for your portfolio in your thirties and forties isn't right for you when you're nearing retirement or already retired. Regular reassessment and rebalancing of your portfolio is critical to your financial health in retirement.

CHAPTER EIGHT

Why We Joined Forces with the Retirement Income Source

What drew us to buy into the Retirement Income Source business model? Really, it was that their philosophy was so aligned with our own. Before we were a couple, we had worked together as colleagues, and discovered we had a shared sense of mission. Helping people have better, more secure lives in retirement was important to both of us, and we were passionate about what we did for a living. We bonded over discussing the conflicts we had with the financial industry as it existed; how advisors were incentivized and paid, the kinds of investments people were being funneled into, and how these things could be done better. We combined our businesses together—and as we are building our business, this allows us to build our relationship together as well.

We both saw a need in the market that wasn't being fulfilled. The vast majority of financial advisors are growth specialists. But we could see the need for people to understand the wisdom of investing for income, and we couldn't understand why others in our profession weren't doing it too. It was common sense, so why were we seemingly the only ones who got it?

That changed when we met some others who saw eye to eye with us and led to the founding of the Retirement Income Source. How strongly did we believe in our mission? We became stockholders in the franchise and are on the board. We're active in coaching, training, and mentoring elite advisors in this philosophy and helping them to provide the very best to their clients.

LINDSEY

We loved Retirement Income Source and everything they provided to us; they had amazing ethics and a terrific philosophy on investing for income, working with the niche of clients who were at the point in their lives when that was especially important. As independent franchisers we work with advisors who are uniquely well qualified in the retirement income area. We benefit from their national reach and expert insights, and so do our clients.

Through the Retirement Income Source, we're part of a national market study group. We all get together a couple of times a year to study, learn, and discuss the economy, interest rates, stock market history, and current events with experts in the industry. This association provides us with a group of like-minded people with whom to share ideas; we don't always agree with each other, but it brings up everyone's level of knowledge and insight to discuss these issues with forty other franchisees who share a philosophy about investing. That's many years' worth of experience for all of us to draw upon. We're still independent business owners but our relationship with the Retirement Income Source allows us access to valuable proprietary tools and continuing education. Continuing education for us is at least as important as it is for our clients, and we'd be remiss if we didn't seek out those kinds of opportunities.

NATHAN

If you're going to be excellent at what you do, you have to surround yourself with excellent people. You know, I grew up playing baseball, I coached baseball, and I coached some very successful teams. Good players want to play for good teams, and they want to contribute to the team to make it even better. They want to surround themselves with other deeply committed people, to help promote those people and educate those around them because it benefits everyone. That's how I feel about joining up with the Retirement Income Source. As someone who believes in bringing his "A" game to whatever I do, it made sense to me.

The training doesn't stop with us; our staff is also coached and trained by the company in office management, customer service skills, and communication, the better to serve you.

We Bring Other Experts to the Table

We work with other experts in related fields—estate planning and tax experts—so that the right hand always knows what the left hand is doing, and you don't have to worry about communication flowing between those who are working for you.

We firmly believe that the Retirement Income Source brings value, not just to us but to our clients, on so many levels.

In Conclusion...

We'd love to talk with you, even if you've got an advisor you are happy with, and have no intention of changing at this point. Our foundation is built on the idea of educating people about retirement and income, and it's more than a job for us; it's a mission, and we're all in.

The investment strategies we use aren't new; they worked for many people for many years. It wasn't until the '80s that investing for growth and taking unnecessary or speculative risks became the new norm. Taking risks with your assets is a fairly new concept in comparison to the time-tested strategies of investing for income. But it's far from being the best way.

We'd welcome the chance to tell you more, and there's no pressure on you to become a client. It's got to be a good fit in both directions. The important thing is that you're informed about your options and can make educated choices about what you want and need in retirement.

You can connect with us in a lot of ways. Register for our webinars, workshops, or seminars on our website; you may also schedule a consultation, listen to our radio show, and so much more. To find us on the Retirement Income Source, visit https://theretirementincomestore. com/income-specialist/lindsey-cotter-and-nathan-cox/.

For anyone who wants to know more about retirement planning, we cover topics like Social Security, required minimum distribution, estate planning, common mistakes investors make, and a lot more. We've got a newsletter you can sign up to receive. We do frequent in-person seminars and live webinars too if you'd like to be able to ask questions, and those are listed on our website as well.

Give a listen to our radio show! It's a lively weekly exchange of views on all topics related to retirement income and savings. We take questions from callers and you can learn a lot.

Your Victory Lap

We've covered a lot of topics in this book and given you plenty of food for thought. But wherever you are in life's marathon of saving for retirement, the main thing we want to leave you with is this: don't be afraid to ask for help. Don't be afraid to ask questions, even if you aren't sure what questions you ought to ask. So often people don't seek the advice they need because they're afraid that they'll say something that makes them look foolish or uninformed. But a good financial advisor isn't going to make you feel dumb. They're going to do their very best to make complex ideas clear for you, because a good financial advisor sees you as a partner, not just someone handing over their savings for investment. They want you to understand what they're doing, and to make informed choices. Anyone who brushes off your questions or suggests subtly that you can just leave it all in their hands is not doing their job and doesn't deserve your trust. Ultimately your savings are your responsibility. You're the one who's going to live with the consequences of the choices that are made, good or bad, so it's important for you to be an active participant in the planning process, not just an onlooker. We want your retirement to be your Victory Lap!

Printed in the USA
CPSIA information can be obtained
at www.ICGtesting.com
LVHW042037120524
779653LV00001B/4/J